Kerri Sackville narrowly missed out on Hollywood superstardom when she was runner-up to Nicole Kidman for the lead role in *BMX Bandits*. Though she later starred in a TV miniseries, her acting career faltered when she was unable to keep away from the catering table.

Kerri went on to university, and over the next decade worked variously as a social worker, headhunter, admin assistant and – for one brief, bizarre period – a weight loss consultant.

After the birth of her second child, Kerri began writing about the daily crises of her life as a working mum and wife. She is now a blogger, columnist and freelancer whose work has appeared in numerous publications, including *The Sydney Morning Herald*, *The Age*, *The Telegraph* and *Notebook Magazine*.

Kerri's blog, Life and Other Crises, explores a wide range of issues, from sex, parenting, friendship and marriage, to housework, PMS and whether white chocolate is actually chocolate (which, of course, it is not). She is also a regular contributor to the hugely popular website Mamamia.

Kerri lives in Sydney with her architect husband, their three children and an accident-prone rabbit. When she is not writing, looking after the kids or cleaning the house, she enjoys tweeting, drinking caffeine with friends and lying extremely still on the couch.

# When My Husband Does the Dishes

### (He usually wants sex!)

First published in Australia in 2011 by Ebury Press.

This edition published in Great Britain in 2012 by
The Robson Press, an imprint of Biteback Publishing Ltd
Westminster Tower
3 Albert Embankment
London
SE1 7SP
Copyright © Kerri Sackville 2011

ISBN 978-1-84954-181-7

10 9 8 7 6 5 4 3 2 1

A CIP catalogue record for this book is available from the British Library.

Set in Dolly and Dancing Script OT by Namkwan Cho
Cover design by Namkwan Cho

Printed and bound in Great Britain by CPI Group (UK) Ltd, Croydon CR0 4YY

*For Tony, Arkie, Saachi and Calliope. My family.*

'I love you, Mama. But you are very stupid.'
Toddler

'Lamb chops come from lambs? But why do we eat our friends?'
Pinkela

'I have to be perfectly honest, Mum.
That dress makes you look horrible.'
Little Man

'What's your plan for my shirts? If you leave them on the
floor long enough, will the gravity of the earth iron them?'
The Architect

# Contents

# A ~~Bit~~ Quite a Lot About the Author

I have written this book for people like me, people who can relate to me, or people who find me amusing. Which, in a tragic sort of way, I am.

So here is a bit about me.

I am in my early forties, which means I feel about twenty-five on some days and eighty-three on others.

I am a mum. I have three kids: an eleven-year-old boy, a nine-year-old girl, and a completely insane toddler (who is also a girl, but her insanity takes precedence over her gender at this point).

I have one husband, The Architect. He is not insane, but he frequently drives me insane, as I do him, so it's a nicely symbiotic relationship.

I have many friends who make me feel good about myself.

I have numerous acquaintances, some of whom make me feel good about myself and others who make me feel very small.

I cook, clean, run the household, pay the bills, and arrange our social lives.

I work from home as a writer in the twelve minutes free I have each day.

And in the past several years, I have done all of the following:

- *Sworn in front of my children.*
- *Responded, 'I hate you, too' to my angry son.*
- *Responded, 'Here, I'll call her for you' when said son informed me he wanted to go and live with Nana.*
- *Answered, 'From God,' when my daughter asked me where babies came from, even though I am aware of the somewhat more technical explanation.*
- *Locked myself in the bathroom to read.*
- *Locked myself in the bathroom to cry.*
- *Screamed at my husband for no reason other than that I was exhausted and cranky.*
- *Accidentally maimed two of my children, one wound requiring several plasters, the other requiring several stitches.*
- *Fed my kids noodles and tomato sauce every night for a week.*
- *Fed my toddler chips to keep her quiet in the shopping trolley (but only because she got sick of chocolate).*
- *Agonised over the state of my pores.*
- *Failed to take my children to swimming lessons because I simply couldn't be bothered.*
- *Let my kids watch four hours of TV in a row because I was just over it.*
- *Allowed my house to get into such a state of disarray that it took a full eight hours to get it tidy again.*
- *Eaten jars and jars of Nutella.*
- *Written out my children's homework answers for them because we were all exhausted and starving.*
- *Bribed my children.*
- *Threatened my children.*

- *Smacked my children (then regretted it one second later).*
- *Counted down the minutes till wine o'clock.*
- *Fell asleep in my chair when I was supposed to be working.*
- *Had my phone service cancelled after forgetting to pay the bill.*
- *Cheated at Monopoly so that I could lose quicker and get the game over with.*
- *Realised I hadn't read a book to my youngest child in weeks.*
- *Realised I hadn't fed my kids fruit in days.*
- *Fantasised regularly about Simon Baker, the cute dad from school, and the barista who makes my coffee.*
- *Watched in horror as my child told a complete stranger that his bum was itchy.*
- *Locked my child in the car by accident.*
- *Felt a surge of elation when the school holidays ended.*
- *Pretended to be asleep to avoid sex.*
- *Thought I could quite happily go the rest of my life without ever having sex again.*
- *Felt jealous of my friend's perfect children.*
- *Felt smug about my friend's nightmare children.*
- *Felt murderously resentful of my husband.*
- *Felt deeply grateful to my husband.*
- *Seethed with anger at my kids.*
- *Ached with love for my kids.*
- *Thought, 'Oh. My. God. What have I done?'*

If you can relate to any of the above, then this book is for you.

And if you can't, then I respect and applaud you. But please don't ever approach me in the street. Our meeting will be rather awkward; you see, I don't actually believe that you exist.

# Part One: Him

## 150 Years With One Person

# My Husband Is a Caramel

*I* like being married. It suits me. I like knowing that I have a regular date for Saturday nights, provided, of course, that we can find a babysitter. I like having someone to talk to every evening. I don't even need my husband to talk back; I just need him to sit there in my general proximity as I prattle on. I like knowing there's at least one person who'll remember my birthday every year, if I remind him repeatedly in the weeks leading up to the big day. I like having someone to cuddle when I feel like it (quite often), have sex with when I feel like it (slightly less often), and to massage my feet when I feel like it (every single day, although sadly he obliges only on my birthday).

Oh, and I quite like The Architect. Well, you know. Most of the time.

My husband and I met about 150 years ago, at university. He was a brilliant Architecture student, and I was a rather less brilliant Arts student who drank coffee and ate finger buns while trying to work out what to do with my life. My husband wore white Don Johnson suits and drove a rattly Suzuki Sierra; I wore green and purple and avoided him for three days after our first kiss, unsure whether I liked him enough to take it further. I did, of course, and fell madly in love with his intellect, his humour, his tormented-genius aura, and his remarkable similarity to Michael J. Fox.

Apart from a brief break (using 'brief' in the sense of 'nearly seven years'), we've been together ever since.

Since then, The Architect has given me three incredible children, who are the epicentre of my universe. He also provides me with opportunities to leave these incredible children when I need to run screaming out of the house, which occurs fairly regularly. So far so good.

However, marriage, for all its wonderful qualities, is extremely challenging. Consider what marriage involves in the twenty-first century. Two people vow to stay together for the rest of their lives, having no idea how long those lives will actually last. And lives these days can last a long time. The Architect and I married when I was twenty-nine, which is not particularly young, but I could conceivably have up to seventy years of marriage all up. And that's the thing. If we only lived thirty or forty years, marriage wouldn't be so difficult. But ninety or 100 years? That's a hell of a long time to spend with one person.

So what does marriage mean?

Well, marriage is about agreeing to forsake sexual intimacy with all others. Forever. No matter how cute the others might be. No matter how shapely their arms, no matter how sexy the tattoo on their right shoulderblade, no matter how thick and lustrous their blond hair. No matter whether they are George Clooney, or Simon Baker, or the barista at the cafe. They are not permitted.

Emotional intimacy with members of the opposite sex must also be carefully controlled so that it doesn't 'cross the line'. No one is precisely sure where that line actually is, but we all agree it is there.

Furthermore, the married couple undertakes to be together every single day, seven days a week, 365 days a year, whether they feel like it or not. They agree to share a bathroom, pool finances, hang with each other's families and friends, and even produce other, new people, who possess half of one's genes and half of the other's.

It is a huge ask.

Marriage is a commitment to having one person meet all your companionship needs *forever*. It's great in theory, but ridiculously demanding, if not near impossible, in practice. Marriage – traditional marriage, anyway – is like being only allowed one book to read for the rest of your life. Or one hairstyle to wear. Or even one car to drive. It won't matter how perfectly suited you are to it now, how wholly it seems to meet your needs. After fifteen or twenty years, that Don Johnson suit/Suzuki Sierra/tormented-genius aura is going to seem very, very old.

People grow and change, and what makes a partner ideal at the age of twenty may not seem equally as ideal twenty years down the track. After all, being attracted to someone, say, for their cute white suit and the love you two share for West Coast Coolers (did I mention The Architect and I met in the 1980s?) will not help you through the good times and bad. And though it's great fun mending the broken soul of a tormented genius when you're eighteen or twenty, this does not auger well for long-term marital success, particularly when baby tormented geniuses come along.

You see, taste changes as you age and mature. To use a food metaphor, right up until my late thirties, I was totally into sweets: chocolates, lollies and ice-cream with hot fudge sauce. Then suddenly, after my third child was born, I started craving salty foods. All the time. Instead of wanting caramels after dinner, I wanted cheese. Instead of making a cup of tea with honey to drink with my sandwich, I made soup. There was nothing wrong with sweets. They were still as objectively delicious and finely made as ever before. I'd just gone off them for a while. I really, really craved a different flavour.

My husband is a caramel. If you know what I mean.

Now, just because you have cravings for different tastes doesn't mean you have to go out and eat at a foreign restaurant. And, obviously couples can work at growing together, or at least accepting and accommodating each other's differences and changing needs. However, people will always, always, *always* want what they don't have – even if only fleetingly, or in the company of others. If your partner is strong and stoic, at some point you're going to long for vulnerable and soft. If he is ambitious and hardworking, you'll pine for relaxed and easygoing. If he looks like Michael J. Fox, you'll want Bruce Willis.

It's human nature. And a lifetime is a long time to have just the one taste.

## The Wife's Lament: If Only He...

- ↳ *Had a bigger bank account.*
- ↳ *Was more generous with his money.*
- ↳ *Stopped wasting all of our money.*
- ↳ *Spent more time with me.*
- ↳ *Didn't hang around me all the time.*
- ↳ *Was more career focused.*
- ↳ *Focused less on his career and more on his family.*
- ↳ *Had more hair.*
- ↳ *Shaved his beard.*

- Had a broader physique.
- Lost weight.
- Had a bigger penis.
- Had a longer penis.
- Knew what to do with his penis.
- Was gentler in bed.
- Took charge in bed.
- Took longer than three minutes.
- Got it over with in three minutes.
- Found some more friends.
- Ditched his stupid friends.
- Took care of his appearance.
- Stopped spending hours in front of the mirror.
- Was more handy.
- Would call a tradesman once in a while.
- Stopped indulging the kids.
- Wasn't so hard on the kids.
- Was more affectionate.
- Was less possessive.
- Was more of a bloke.
- Wasn't such a bloody bloke.

# Can't Live with Him but Fell in Love

*I* love my husband. I love men in general. In fact, I have had romantic interest in various men for as long as I can remember. One of my earliest memories is of sitting on the steps of my preschool, praying to God not to let Leo Whitman leave to go overseas with his parents. Sadly Leo did leave, which no doubt contributed to my later atheism. And though you couldn't really classify the relationship as 'love' – particularly when the four-year-old in question was not actually aware that we were in a relationship – I do believe it was my first experience of heartbreak.

Still, as much as I find men attractive, I also find them extremely challenging to live with. Of course, as I am only living with one man at present, I am using the term 'them' in the sense of 'The Architect'. However, I do know from having conducted careful research – that is, talking to my girlfriends and mother – that other women find living with their husbands challenging, too.

(To be fair, my male friends inform me that women are also extremely challenging, but for the purposes of this book, these assertions are completely irrelevant.)

I fell in love with The Architect for his intellect, his wit, and the special smile he gave me from the front seat of his car on one of our early dates. I was thrilled when we first moved in together. I wanted his intellect, his wit, and his special smile to be with me all the time. And I got them. I live with a highly intelligent man who can answer pretty much any question I throw at him. He makes me laugh, all the time. ('This meat is so tough,' he texted recently from a boring business dinner. 'Oh wait, it was my arm. I was gnawing it.') And when he smiles, he lifts our whole family. But what I didn't realise is that my husband's marvellous qualities come with a whole lot of rather less marvellous ones. Eccentricities. Irritating habits. Episodes of thoughtlessness. Mess. And extraordinarily loud bouts of throat clearing. And while I have become rather more habituated to The Architect's wonderful qualities over the years, his less endearing qualities continue to bother me more and more.

## It Makes Me Crazy When My Husband...

- Leaves the toilet seat up.
- Drinks the juice straight from the container.
- Returns my car with no petrol in it.
- Returns my car with a dent in it.
- Returns my car with no wing mirror on it (and then tells me it was my fault because I didn't leave enough space for him to park).
- Wakes me up to tell me Toddler is crying.
- Wakes me up to tell me that there is a 'funny noise' and that I should 'go and investigate'.
- Leaves huge, crusted pieces of food on his plate when putting it in the dishwasher.
- Adds paprika to my pot roast, gives it a stir then takes full credit for the meal.

- Tells me the schnitzel I cooked was 'fine' but 'not as good as Auntie Anna's schnitzel'.
- Keeps his shoes on when lying on the freshly made bed.
- Doesn't read the texts I send him.
- Doesn't read the emails I send him.
- Pushes me aside and jumps into the shower just as I'm ready to hop in.
- 'Tidies up' by throwing things into the nearest available drawer, even if the thing is a can of tuna and the drawer belongs to socks.
- 'Makes the bed' by throwing the covers over whatever happens to be lying on the bed, even if what happens to be lying on the bed is a pair of his shoes.
- Proposes buying a boat with a friend, despite us being flat broke.
- Proposes taking the kids to Disneyland, despite us being flat broke.
- Proposes buying himself a new car despite us being flat broke.
- Says vaguely, 'Oh, we'll work it out somehow' when I ask where the money is coming from.
- Engages the kids in a pillow-fight five minutes before they're meant to go to sleep.
- Collects parking fines like they are swap cards.
- Leaves sideburn clippings in the sink.
- Leaves toenail clippings on the floor.
- Bathes Toddler then presents her to me for dressing.
- Tells me I look 'fine' when I ask how I look.
- Tells me something awful has happened at work but refuses to tell me what.
- Tells me I'm in a bad mood. Even when I am. Especially when I am.

# Can't Sleep with Him but It's His Bed Too

*O*ne of the many benefits to marriage is having someone to cuddle up with at night – or at least to lie beside, companionably, while watching TV. One of the many disadvantages, however, is not being able to kick them out of bed afterwards.

Yes, sharing a bed is one of the great compromises of marital life. I have never quite understood why falling in love and getting married means relinquishing my right to fling my legs around unobstructed, or to have a full night's sleep without being woken by the sound of frantic throat clearing three centimetres from my ear.

Don't get me wrong. I like sharing a room with my husband. He travels a lot, and when I get into bed alone at the end of the day I actually feel quite bereft. What's more, I like *using* a bed with my husband (provided I'm not too tired, the kitchen is clean, and all the kids are asleep). At the end of the evening, though, I would prefer for us to have a nice hug then move to twin beds and slumber – separately, but together – for the rest of the night.

I'm all for the concept of sleeping in the same bed as one's partner – in theory, anyway. It's just the practicalities that

concern me. I'm a light sleeper, and The Architect ... well ...
he *bothers* me. He rolls over in bed. (I know – how selfish is
that?) He breathes, heavily at times. (I know – inconsiderate
again!) He pulls the covers up. He pushes the covers down. He
scratches himself. And he clears his throat. Of course, from
the other side of the room, his throat clearing isn't so bad. But
from his position next to my ear, it's like being woken by a
volcano erupting in my head. At three in the morning. Every.
Single. Morning.

Furthermore, I like a lot of personal space. I like to sleep in
different positions: on my back, on my tummy, with my arms
behind my head, arms to my sides, arms straight up in the air
(okay, not really, but I'd prefer to keep the option open), legs
splayed, knees drawn up to my chest, hanging from the chan-
delier wearing bunny ears and a fluffy tail. (Nah, I'm lying
about that last one. It's my husband's fantasy.) And I don't
like to be restricted in my movements by anyone pushing my
limbs out of the way when I fancy a good stretch.

What's more, it's not just in the physical realm that sharing a bed can be problematic. The Architect and I do, on
occasion, have little arguments (using 'on occasion' in the
sense of 'often' and 'little' in the sense of 'medium to big'),
and after one of these arguments, having to sleep in the same
bed together is most annoying.

(Of course, according to the television shows, the husband
is supposed to sleep on the couch after a fight with his wife.
However, The Architect just rolls his eyes when I attempt to
expel him from our marital bed and settles back under the
covers. Now, *I'm* certainly not going to go and sleep on the
couch, as I have a bad back, and besides, why the hell should I?
So I generally curl up into a tiny ball at the extreme edge of the
bed in order to demonstrate just how cross I am. The Architect

doesn't notice, as he's generally fast asleep by then, but at least I feel like I'm making my point.)

## My Husband's Bedtime Crimes

- *Pushing me away when I accidentally brush his limbs. I have no desire to touch him in the middle of the night, but I like sleeping like a starfish. I don't know why. I just do.*
- *Insisting on turning the air conditioner down so low that our room has the temperature of an Arctic weather station. I am aware that men and women have different body temperatures, but perhaps the fact that I am wearing long-sleeved pyjamas, woolly socks and a fleece hoodie is an indication that it is a touch too cold for comfort?*
- *Watching television till midnight every night. Even when he uses headphones so that I can't hear the sound, I can still see the screen flashing. And speaking of television, I don't understand why he loves motorcycle programmes so much. He doesn't have a motorcycle.*
- *Insisting that I turn the television off when he is ready for sleep, on the very rare occasions that I want to stay up a little later.*
- *Rearranging his bedding after I've gone to sleep. It disturbs me. I know he's uncomfortable, but I figure he's made his bed, now he'll just have to lie in it.*
- *Lying in bed coughing and spluttering all night when he's sick. I mean, I'm very sorry that the poor man is ill, but can't he just be ill on the couch?*
- *Clearing his throat. He should hold on till morning.*
- *Blowing his nose. Ditto.*
- *Leaving used tissues in the bed. Do I need to say more?*

- ■ *Setting the alarm for five a.m. so he can get to work early. I understand his meeting is important, but so is my rest. Sleep on the couch.*

- ■ *Approaching me for sex when I'm already asleep. And if my eyes are closed, I am asleep. Try again tomorrow.*

# No, You're Not Losing Your Hair

*O*ne of the greatest differences between men and women is tact. Women have it in spades, men ... not so much.

Women can be extremely tactful, which is highly advantageous in marriage, as there is an enormous amount to be tactful about. We are diplomatic and considerate in our dealings with other people, carefully moderating the truth to avoid hurting feelings or creating awkward situations (also known as 'getting ourselves into trouble'). Now, a man might call a woman's expression of tact 'lying', which if you look at it from a very narrow perspective, it technically is. However, men, as we know, think in Black and White, and do not understand the multiple Shades of Grey that permeate relationships.

I try to be scrupulously honest in my relationship with The Architect. I do. But because of my extreme tact and diplomacy, I fail. You see, if I really was scrupulously honest, then he'd know that he is losing his hair, that the new jacket he bought himself looks ridiculous, that I have a huge crush on a father from school, that I use his toothbrush all the time in the shower, and that I spend way too much money on clothes.

But I'm not lying. I'm being considerate. I have to. It's a question of marital survival.

## ~~Lies Wives Tell~~ Things Considerate Wives Say

- 'No, you're not losing your hair.'
- 'No, I hadn't really noticed that you're losing your hair.'
- 'No, I don't care that you're losing your hair.'
- 'No, this isn't new. I've had it for ages!'
- 'Oh, this? It was really cheap.'
- 'Oh, this? My mum bought it for me.'
- 'No, I don't think your brother is cute.'
- 'No, I don't think your friend is cute.'
- 'Well, yes, he's a bit cute, but he's not my type.'
- 'No, I wasn't flirting!'
- 'No, I never think about my ex-boyfriend.'
- 'Oh, it's huge.'
- 'It's definitely above average.'
- 'It's totally normal.'
- 'No, size doesn't matter!'
- 'Yes, of course I like your mother.'
- 'Yes, of course my mother likes you.'
- 'No, I never complain to my mother about you.'
- 'No, I never complain to my friends about you.'
- 'No, I never talk to my friends about our sex life.'
- 'Oh, you definitely could have been a professional skier if it wasn't for that injury.'
- 'Oh, you definitely could have been a famous rock star if only you'd joined a band.'
- 'No, I don't mind you quitting your job in order to take a year off to "find yourself".'
- 'Oh yes, of course I believe you are terribly ill. A normal temperature doesn't mean anything.'
- 'No, I have no idea what happened to that bottle of wine.'
- 'No, I have no idea what happened to your favourite ice-cream.'

🥿 'No, I didn't use your razor on my legs.'

🥿 'Yes, of course I paid the electricity bill.'

🥿 'Yes, of course I dropped your suit at the drycleaner.'

🥿 'Yes, you are astonishingly good at barbecuing. Truly. Nobody else comes close.'

🥿 'I've got my period. Yes, still.'

🥿 'I've got an awful headache.'

🥿 'Oh, this? It's … er … a back massager.'

🥿 'No, I didn't fall asleep.'

🥿 'Oh, absolutely I was thinking about you.'

🥿 'Yes, I had a huge orgasm.'

🥿 'No, it doesn't matter that I didn't have an orgasm.'

🥿 'I have been playing with the kids all day.'

🥿 'No, I'm not on Twitter. I'm working.'

🥿 'I want you to be completely honest – how do I look?'

# When My Husband Does the Dishes He Wants Sex

*M*en's version of the truth is somewhat different to women's. You see, men don't openly ~~lie~~ stretch the truth like women do. In their minds, they are being completely honest. To men, there is Truth ('It's horrible'), Lying ('Sure, if you want me to say it's nice, it's nice') or Not Buying Into It ('No chance am I answering that one'). And we all know what Not Buying Into It means. He hates it.

Although men may not deliberately tell fibs, they certainly do not speak the truth, the whole truth and nothing but the truth. There is a rich subtext to men's language, an underlying hidden message beneath even the most innocuous of utterances. It's not a particularly complex subtext, though, and it is not too difficult to decode. It took me about three months into my relationship with The Architect to work his out, and since then, it's all just been variations on a theme.

You see, with men, it's not about what they say. It's about everything they don't.

| What My Husband Says | What My Husband Means |
| --- | --- |
| *'I never spend any money on myself.'* | *'... unless you count watches, cars, flat screen TVs and iPhones. Which I don't.'* |
| *'I'm sick.'* | *'Okay, so I don't actually have a temperature, and I don't have any symptoms other than a general feeling of malaise, but believe me, I am desperately ill. And even though you have a forty-degree fever yet are cooking the kids' dinner and supervising their homework, I can't possibly get up to help you as I am so terribly poorly.'* |
| *'What did you do all day?'* | *'Why is the house such a mess?'* |
| *'Oh, this show? It's a documentary.'* | *'... about the porn industry.'* |
| *'Oh, this show? It's a foreign language film.'* | *'... about a lesbian yoga instructor who seduces her female, married neighbour.'* |
| *'Look! I made dinner!'* | *'I cooked my favourite meal and left a hideous mess for you to clean up.'* |
| *'Look! I cooked dinner for you!'* | *'I want sex tonight.'* |
| *'Look! I did all the dishes!'* | *'I want sex tonight.'* |
| *'Look! I put the kids to bed!'* | *'I want sex tonight.'* |
| *'It's a business trip. I'll be working the whole time.'* | *'... except when we go for that long lunch on Tuesday, on that golfing trip on Wednesday, and to that fancy restaurant on Thursday night.'* |

Kerri Sackville

| What My Husband Says | What My Husband Means |
| --- | --- |
| 'I know exactly where I'm going.' | 'I am completely and utterly lost, but would rather chew off my own arm than ask for directions.' |
| 'One sec, okay? I just want to get the cricket score.' | 'Cancel your plans. I'm going to be glued to the set for the next four hours.' |
| 'Is this what we're having for dinner?' | 'Where on earth is the meat?' |
| 'I'll do it in a second.' | 'I'll do it in the next few hours. Maybe.' |
| 'I'll do it in a minute.' | 'I'll do it sometime today, but more likely tomorrow.' |
| 'I'll do it tomorrow.' | 'I'll do it sometime in the distant, indefinite future.' |
| 'I'll do it later.' | 'I have no intention of ever doing it.' |
| 'This chicken doesn't taste like Auntie Anna's schnitzel.' | 'I don't like this schnitzel, I want Auntie Anna's schnitzel.' |
| 'The baby's crying.' | 'Go fix the baby.' |
| 'Where are all my clean shirts?' | 'Why haven't you done the laundry?' |
| 'We're out of toothpaste!' | 'Why haven't you bought some toothpaste?' |
| 'Yes, yes, you look fine.' | 'I haven't actually looked at you.' |
| 'You look nice, okay?' | 'Finish getting dressed. We need to leave now.' |
| 'If you like it, wear it.' | 'That outfit is hideous.' |
| 'Ooh, you look great.' | 'I want to have sex tonight.' |
| 'I'll be home in five minutes.' | 'I'll be home within the hour.' |

| What My Husband Says | What My Husband Means |
|---|---|
| *'I'll be home around seven.'* | *'I could be home anytime between seven and ten.'* |
| *'I've invited the new guy over. You'll love him.'* | *'You'll despise him with a passion but I don't want to hear about it.'* |
| *'Do you want a massage?'* | *'I want to have sex.'* |
| *'Come to bed.'* | *'I want to have sex.'* |
| *'Are you asleep?'* | *'I want to have sex.'* |
| *'I love you.'* | *'I want to have sex.'* |

*Sexy Time*

# Sleep Is Better Than Sex

As a mother my life has become a juggling act, a frantic dance between competing priorities. There is simply no downtime, no moments when I can clock off and not be a parent anymore. Even when the kids are asleep I am on call. I am never, ever, off duty.

The days when I manage to get everything ticked off my To Do list are infrequent. The days when I manage to get everything ticked off my To Do list and get the kids to sleep with time to spare before collapsing from exhaustion are rare indeed (using 'rare' in the sense of 'has never actually happened to me, but I'm working on it'). And when I do have a few precious moments of free time, well, I don't want to take off my grotty clothes and make passionate love. I want to sleep. For as long as possible.

It's sad but it's true. In the pre-parenthood Hierarchy of Needs, sex may be up there alongside food, shelter and watching *MasterChef* as one of the key priorities in life. Post-parenthood, however, everything changes. Sleep –

rare, precious sleep – shoots to the top of the list, rivalled only by oxygen as the most sought-after commodity in the maternal world.

No matter how handsome your partner is, no matter how high your libido, you will never crave sex like you crave sleep after a baby. Many women I know have sobbed with exhaustion, desperate for a nap. And yet I don't know any who have sobbed with lust, desperate for a shag. It's true that sex can be incredibly rewarding, particularly with a skilful partner. The reality, though, is that sleep is even better, and you can do it all on your own. Now obviously sex can be had in all sorts of places, and in numerous, even uncomfortable, positions. You can have sex on the floor, against a tree, in a car, on a chair, on a kitchen bench, even in a pool (although, to be honest, the pool option has never worked for me. I keep floating away).

But sleep can be had absolutely anywhere, too – and far more easily and quickly than sex. Since I've had kids, I've slept in innumerable places – pretty much anywhere I've lain my head for more than ten seconds. It's got to the point where I fall asleep every time I am horizontal, like one of those dollies that closes its eyes every time you lay it down.

And unlike sex, I can sleep in public and no one will raise an eyebrow. In recent months, I've slept at the movies, on my mother's couch, on my girlfriend's shoulder, on the train, at my desk, and on our living room floor. No one was bothered in the slightest, except for my girlfriend (when I started to dribble on her) and Toddler, who inserted her finger in my nose to wake me up.

I can't imagine the same level of acceptance with public sex. Even if I did have the motivation to try. Which I don't, of course. I'm way too tired.

# Why I Prefer Sleep

- 👙 Sleeping can't get me pregnant.
- 👙 There is no mess to clean up after sleeping.
- 👙 I can sleep all by myself, without the need for my husband or toys.
- 👙 I can sleep with my friends without anyone getting hurt.
- 👙 I can sleep with several people at once without damaging my reputation.
- 👙 Sleep doesn't require me to shave my legs or smell particularly good.
- 👙 When I sleep it doesn't matter if I've forgotten to brush my teeth.
- 👙 I can sleep even when I'm really tired. Actually, being tired is a distinct advantage.
- 👙 I can sleep even if I'm annoyed with my husband.
- 👙 I never need to introduce new tricks to keep sleep exciting.
- 👙 I don't need to remove any clothes to sleep.
- 👙 If I have a really bad sleep, I don't need to pretend it was good.
- 👙 I don't need my husband to enjoy the sleep.
- 👙 I don't need to convince my husband he's great at sleeping.
- 👙 I can sleep even when I've got my period.
- 👙 Sleeping can't give me a painful leg cramp or a urinary tract infection.
- 👙 There's no shame in announcing that I'm great at sleeping.
- 👙 I can sleep at the movies. Even kids' movies. Especially kids' movies.
- 👙 I can keep my nose pore strip on while I'm sleeping.
- 👙 I can keep my mouthguard in while I'm sleeping.
- 👙 I don't need to worry about whether other people are sleeping more frequently than me.
- 👙 I don't need to worry about other people catching me sleeping (unless it's my husband and we're having sex).
- 👙 The kids won't be traumatised if they see me sleeping.
- 👙 My parents already know that I sleep.

# How to Kill a Mood

The problem with marital sex isn't just one of exhaustion. Sex in a long-term relationship is simply not as exciting as it is when you are first dating. And when you are dealing with the additional challenges of parenthood, the excitement can wane even further.

The issue is, of course, one of familiarity. To maintain sizzling sexual chemistry you need to retain a little mystery. You do not need to know everything about your partner; rather, too much information is the natural enemy of desire. You don't need to see your partner on the toilet. You don't need to see the stuff that comes out of his nose. And you certainly don't need to hear that disgusting noise he makes in the back of his throat at night. The same, no doubt, is true of women. After all, even Angelina or Scarlett would be less irresistible with a shower cap on her head, baby's snot on her arm, a wet nappy in her hand and a pore strip on her nose.

But herein lies the problem. It is impossible for us mothers to be mysterious, unless we pay someone else to look after our offspring.

For a start, children rob us of our inhibition. (And they certainly don't keep it for themselves, as I learned when my son proudly invited the world to, 'Look at my big penis!')

28

Before children, for example, I was very private about my breasts. I revealed them to a select few, and only in very intimate moments, none of which took place in parks or shopping centres (or at least, very few of them did). After breastfeeding three babies, however, my breasts have become as private and sacred as the pair of old socks they now resemble. Toddler could be painting my boobs fire-engine red and I'd barely notice, so accustomed am I to my chest being public property.

And it's not just my breasts that are on display. Toilet time, too, has become a shared experience over the years. My kids are fascinated with bodily functions and don't much like closed doors, so my business is frequently conducted in full view of the entire family. And though my older kids are now more respectful of personal space, Toddler asserts her inalienable right to follow me everywhere, and to cuddle me at absolutely any moment. So I sit on the toilet with her ten centimetres from my face, talking, asking questions and monitoring the procedure. It's not ideal, but it's better than her climbing on my lap, which is where she wants to be.

Now I realise that public toileting is the surest way to destroy mystery in a marriage. However, I've grown so used to being observed that I barely remember to close the door when friends come over, let alone when it's just my husband and me. It's not that I'm an exhibitionist. I don't need to have an audience. But an audience doesn't bother me like it should.

It's not just in their actions that children are the enemies of mystery. They also demonstrate an alarming candour with regard to the sharing of information. Just the other day, for example, Toddler matter-of-factly informed a stranger, 'My poo-poo is stuck!' As a mother, I simply have to discuss bums. It's what my kids are interested in.

Of course, I know that it's not necessary to tell my husband every time I do a wee. I know that, for the sake of romance, some things are better left unsaid. But after a day in which all things bottom are the main topics of conversation, the concept of mystery starts to seem a little remote.

So it's not surprising that when the time comes for sex, we mothers can sometimes hit the wrong note. Or fail to hit a note at all...

## Ways Mums Destroy Sex

- Say, 'Oh, do we have to?'
- Say, 'But we had sex only a week ago!'
- Say, 'Oh, okay, if you really want to.'
- Say, 'Okay, fine, but only if I can keep reading my book.'
- Say, 'Can you make it quick? I'm really tired.'
- Say, 'Can you make it quick? I have to call my mother.'
- In the midst of proceedings, tell him the cute thing the baby said today.
- In the midst of proceedings, tell him you're worried about your son.
- In the midst of proceedings, ask if he remembered to buy nappies on the way home.
- Refer to yourself as Mummy, as in, 'Mummy likes this!'
- Refer to him as Daddy.
- Refer to his penis as his 'pee-pee'.
- Wipe some food off his face with your wet finger.
- Leak breastmilk onto him.
- Ask, 'Do you think it's time to have another baby?'
- Ask, 'Do you think it's time you got a vasectomy?'
- Ask, 'Can you believe how floppy my boobs have got since I stopped breastfeeding?'
- Ask, 'Are you nearly done?'
- Answer, 'It's fine,' when asked if you're enjoying it.

🩲 *Yawn.*

🩲 *Fall asleep.*

🩲 *Wonder out loud whether you've left the oven on.*

🩲 *Wonder out loud why your period is late.*

🩲 *Grumble that your haemorrhoids are bothering you.*

🩲 *Remind him to call his mother.*

🩲 *Say, 'Please don't speak. I'm trying to visualise Simon Baker.'*

# We're Doing It Tomorrow

*N*ow, don't get me wrong. It's not that I don't like sex. Truly. I love sex! After all, it's sex that got me in the motherhood way in the first place. It's just that now that I'm a mother, sex can be a bit like going to the beach. It's lovely when I'm lying on my towel, soaking up the warm rays of the sun. However, it can take quite a lot of time and effort to pack up the car and actually get there, if you know what I mean. And once I'm ready to leave the beach, I'm all hot and sweaty and sticky, and I need to take a shower, and I end up picking sand out of my nether regions for ages.

Ultimately, as pleasurable as the whole exercise is, it can sometimes feel like too much bother, particularly when the kitchen needs tidying, the school lunches haven't been made, and I'm longing for a nap.

Still, all these obstacles can be overcome, and a satisfying marital sex session can be achieved. It just takes time. And patience. And compromise. And, on occasion, a raincheck.

# Marital Sex: A Timeline

**8.00:** *I put the kids to bed. This takes approximately an hour and a half, as Pinkela is 'feeling funny'. Little Man is 'too hot' then 'too cold', and Toddler is partying hard in her cot.*

**9.30:** *The Architect switches off the TV and looks at me in that special way that he has done every couple of nights for the past 150 years. 'Come to bed,' he murmurs seductively. I feel my head swimming with exhaustion. 'Can we do it tomorrow?' I ask. 'I'm really tired.' The Architect looks plaintive. 'You told me yesterday we'd do it today,' he says. I sigh. I tell him I've just got to finish washing up the dishes. He tells me he already has. I peer into the sink and it's sparkling. I tell him I just have to check on the children. He tells me to hurry.*

**9.35:** *I check on the kids. They are sleeping soundly. I sigh again and head for the bedroom. It will be nice! I know that. I'm just so tired...*

**9.45:** *I go to my bedroom where The Architect grabs me in a passionate embrace. I disentangle myself and tell him I haven't brushed my teeth yet.*

**9.50:** *I head to the bathroom where I brush and floss my teeth. I consider washing and moisturising my face, but now that I have to have sex I won't possibly have time.*

**9.55:** *I go to bed. I remind The Architect that he hasn't brushed his teeth yet. He goes to the bathroom and returns in two seconds flat.*

**9.56:** *The Architect initiates sex.*

**9.57:** *Within thirty seconds, Pinkela calls from the other room. I become airborne before the second 'm' in 'Mum' has been uttered.*

**9.58:** *I go in to find Pinkela dreaming peacefully. I wait with her for a minute just to be sure. Then I wait with her another minute more.*

**10.00:** *I return to bed. I note with slight disappointment that my husband is still awake, and still keen. We resume activities.*

**10.05:** *I suddenly remember to tell The Architect about the lunch at my parents' place on Sunday. He is momentarily deflated, but rallies.*

**10.07:** *We resume activities. It's actually quite nice, really.*

**10.10:** *My leg suddenly goes into a spasm. I disentangle myself to do some quick stretching exercises. 'Oh, for God's sake,' says The Architect.*

**10.13:** *We resume activities.*

**10.16:** *Toddler starts to cry. We look at each other and groan. 'I'll go,' says The Architect.*

**10.17:** *I rest my head for a moment on the pillow.*

**10.21:** *'What? What?' I exclaim, as The Architect wakes me by nibbling on my ear. 'Oh, were you asleep?' he asks. 'I bet I can wake you up...' He resumes activities. I fall immediately back to sleep.*

**10.22:** *The Architect continues hopefully for a minute before realising it's not going to happen. He sighs, turns on the TV and settles down to watch Girls of the Playboy Mansion. I roll over and continue to slumber.*

**10.25:** *'We're doing it tomorrow,' he says.*

# Dating the Spouse

*N*ow, obviously going on a date without the children is fun. Even a trip to the supermarket without the children is fun these days. But date nights with The Architect can be ... well ... rather underwhelming at times. It's not that they're not enjoyable – they are, truly! It's just that they're never quite as exhilarating as the pre-Married with Children ones were.

I remember the excitement of dating new boyfriends. There was the anticipation of the evening ahead. There were butterflies in my stomach. There was the anxiety about choosing the right clothes, hairstyle and shoes. Where would the evening lead? Would there be a kiss? Would there be a sleepover? Would there be any expression of love? Most importantly, was this man The One?

Dating my husband isn't the same. After all, I know that The Architect is The One. I've been living with him for fifteen years. I wake up with him every morning. I watch him brush his teeth. I put his dirty undies into the washing machine. I think it's understandable if I don't get butterflies at the thought of being alone with him on a Saturday night.

Still, a marital date isn't inferior to a date with a new man. It's just different. More familiar. Less stimulating. Okay, so maybe it's a little bit inferior...

| New Man Date | Marital Date |
| --- | --- |
| *The preparation can be thrilling, if a little bit nerve-racking.* | *The preparation is exhausting. I need to summon up the energy to get dressed and leave the house, having run around after the kids all day. Quite frankly, I'd rather be at home sleeping.* |
| *I look forward to learning more about the new man.* | *I've just seen my man on the toilet. What else is there to learn?* |
| *The date may be expensive, but it's worth it.* | *The date will be ridiculously prohibitive. Not only is there the cost of the evening itself – the movie, the dinner, the drinks, the parking – but there is also the cost of the babysitter. These additional expenses put huge pressure on us both to Have a Good Time ('Are we having forty pounds' worth of fun yet?'), leading to expectations that often cannot be fulfilled.* |
| *When the new man takes out his credit card I will feel happily wined and dined.* | *When The Architect takes out his credit card it is still my money. Besides, we usually pay with my credit card anyway.* |
| *A new man will be happy to take me to the movie of my choice.* | *My husband will want to see what he wants. I'll end up seeing Bruce Willis in Blood And Guts III, while gazing longingly at the poster of Simon Baker in You Could Be My Lover.* |

| New Man Date | Marital Date |
|---|---|
| The date could lead to hours of conversation about everything and anything. | The evening will lead to conversation about the food, the movie and what the kids did that day. After that, we will hit the wall because we know everything about each other already. |
| A good date with a new man lasts till sunrise. | A good date with my husband needs to finish by ten p.m., as the kids will still wake us up at dawn. |
| A date with a new man could leave me giddy with desire and tingling with sexual tension. | A date with my husband could leave me giddy with alcohol, but only if I'm not driving. As for the tingling? Not so much. |
| During a date with a new man, we are both likely to be on our best behaviour. | During a date with my husband, we are likely to end up fighting over who can drink, and who has to drive the babysitter home. |
| A date with a new man may lead to mind-blowing sex. | A date with my husband may lead to marital sex. It will be brief, it will be similar to the sex we've had several hundred times before, and I will be the one responsible for washing the sheets. And his undies. |
| A date with a new man gives rise to exciting possibilities for the future. | A date with my husband gives rise to no exciting possibilities. He will stay over for the night, he will be there the next morning, and chances are he won't ever leave. |
| A date with a new man provides endless fodder for analysis and conversation with your girlfriends. | A date with my husband provides no fodder for conversation with my girlfriends, other than how desperately we need a girls' night out. |

# Bring the Ice-Cream into Bed

*S*ex, one might say, is like ice-cream – if, that is, you like ice-cream. (If you don't, then perhaps substitute something else. Like boiled lollies. Or cheese.)

I love ice-cream. I could eat it most days. Not every day of the week, but frequently. The thing is, though, I don't want the same flavour all of the time. Let's say, for argument's sake, that my husband is chocolate ice-cream. Some days, I really crave a big bowl of chocolate. Other days, however, I find myself longing for vanilla. Occasionally, I hanker for butter pecan. And sometimes, I'm even tempted by rocky road, but only rarely, because I don't really like marshmallows, and now I'm getting off the track...

The point is, when you're married, you can only have one flavour of sex partner all of the time, and this, I find, can be a challenge. Sex therapists will tell you that you can spice up your love life by adding gadgets, lingerie, DVDs, pole dancing, costumes and so on, and to a certain extent this is true. However, to be perfectly honest, no amount of sprinkles and toppings is going to make me feel like chocolate when I'm really craving rum and raisin. If you know what I mean.

Still, there are other options. Some people find that monogamy is simply unworkable and decide to try alternative avenues, such as open marriage. Well, that sounds just marvellous. I can hear The Architect on the phone now: 'Sorry, Kerri, I'm going to be home late tonight. Do you mind feeding and bathing the kids all by yourself? ... No, everything's fine. I'm just having sex with my girlfriend.' Er, no, honey. I don't think so.

The other choice for open-minded couples is swinging, where both partners in the relationship have sex with other people at the same time, with full knowledge. Now, I don't have any problem with swinging. As long as it involves two consenting adults, it sounds like a fine idea.

In principle, anyway.

It's just that ... well ... the technicalities of swinging baffle me. Not, you know, the technicalities of the sex act itself – I'm pretty au fait with all that by now. It's the *organisational* aspect of swinging that I find worrying. How does the whole thing actually work?

I mean, how do two people begin their swinging careers? Do they choose a couple and decide they want to have sex with them? This, to me, immediately poses two distinct problems. For a start, how do you choose a couple? Out of my fairly wide circle of friends, there are virtually no couples of which I would be as willing to have sex with the husband as my own husband would be willing to have sex with the wife. And even if we did stumble upon such a couple, how would we approach them? 'Hi, Jane! Hi, John! We've so greatly enjoyed seeing you at school concerts and the footy, we thought we could all take our clothes off and have intercourse.' Nope. I just can't think of a smooth way to segue into that particular conversation.

The other option, of course, is to join a swingers' club. It's purpose-built and there is no question that the couples who attend are perfectly happy to pop round after dinner for a shag.

But that, too, concerns me. Sure, there will be a lot of couples there, and, sure, there will be a lot of men to choose from. But how do you know that all the good ones won't be taken by the time you get your turn? It would be like being at a party where a box of chocolates is opened and passed around the room. You just *know* that by the time it gets to you, the macadamia centres and hard caramels will be all gone, and you'll be stuck with the horrid orange cream, while no doubt, at the back of the room, your husband is chomping away merrily on a nice mint slice.

Of course, there's the other, equally difficult alternative. It is possible that you will actually score the pick of the bunch (say, the raspberry fondant) and it will be the most delicious thing you've *ever* tasted. And you'll want to come back to the party, time and time again, dying for some more. But the next time you're there, the fondant is being eaten by someone else, or – worse still – the fondant doesn't want to be eaten by you again. This, my friends, would be absolutely heartbreaking.

Or – possibly the most dangerous scenario of all – the fondant is very happy to be eaten by you, and you and the fondant become totally addicted to each other. Before long, you are sneaking out every single night to have a raspberry fondant. In other words, instead of swinging, you are now having an affair.

I have no idea how people can swing, without all the complications and feelings associated with having sex with other people. Kudos to them, but it all sounds too hard for me. I think I'm going to have to just stick with my chocolate swirl.

So how can I deal with eating the same flavour every day (using 'every day' in the sense of 'far, far less frequently than that')? In the end, what it all really boils down to is imagination. Now, obviously I'm brilliantly happy with The Architect just the way he is (using 'brilliantly' in the sense of 'very', 'somewhat', or 'not at all', depending on the day). But for those times when I'm longing for a different flavour, I just use my mind. And my mind is a truly powerful tool. I close my eyes and my brown-haired, clean-shaven, conservative husband can instantly become blond, bearded, bad-assed, broad or Simon Baker. (I'm … er … speaking hypothetically here.) I can give him tattoos, make him grow or shrink, or pierce his eyebrow. I can turn him into a barista, a barrister, a businessman, a surgeon, a fighter pilot, or an underworld biker. I can make him Italian, Swedish, Russian, Irish, Moroccan, or French. (In fact, I often *do* make my husband speak with a French accent. But only because he likes it.)

So for me, it's all about imagination. I can make my man be whoever I want him to be, at that particular moment.

And when all else fails I just bring the ice-cream into bed.

Works every time.

# No Sex, Please – I'm Flirting

*A*s we all know, marriage comes with certain consequences, the most significant being that you are no longer supposed to have sex with anyone else. (Unless, of course, you're a swinger, which, as I have explained, is just too many 'anyone elses' for me.)

Still, no matter how strongly extramarital sex is prohibited, there is one thing that is far harder to thwart. Flirting.

When I was single, flirting was tremendous fun. All that hair tossing, eyelash fluttering and giggling was delicious. And now that I'm married, it still is. Flirting energises me. It makes me feel more attractive. So why do I have to relinquish something so agreeable simply because I have a partner? Why do I have to give up the activity just because I've achieved the goal?

The *Shorter Oxford English Dictionary* (which I keep handy in the kitchen as a booster seat for Toddler) describes flirting as 'behaving superficially in an amorous manner'. And it is this superficiality which is the key. Flirting is superficial. I am not behaving in a deeply or sincerely amorous manner – that is being in love (not a good idea, if the person in question is not my spouse). Neither am I behaving in a physically amorous manner – that is being naked (also not a good idea, unless The Architect agrees, which he is highly unlikely to do). I am just pretending to be amorous. Playing. And it can be great for the spirit.

Ironically, it is only after I mated for life that I became most skilled at flirting. After all, the ability to flirt is based on confidence, and when I knew that at least one person in the world desired me, I became much more self-assured. Now that I actually have a partner, I can flirt for fun rather than necessity, which means that I don't actually need to try. And, given that trying too hard is the death knell of flirting, I can achieve something close to the casual insouciance that characterises a really good flirt.

What's more, when The Architect and I are a bit cranky at each other, flirting can be even more important. A good flirt can give me just the boost I need to make me feel better about myself, a burst of confidence that can only translate into a more positive and healthy relationship. Really, it's a win-win situation.

Of course, it's not a flirting free-for-all. Some basic rules do apply. Generally, happily married men are safer to flirt with than single men (with the exception of waiters, provided that they're half my age and I'm not actually planning to take them home). Gay men are fine, although possibly not quite as satisfying. And unhappily married men are a definite no-go zone, as they'll be convinced that I appreciate them in a way their wife doesn't, and understand them in a way that she's incapable of doing. (And how do you tell a happily married man from an unhappily married man? Well, the happily married man flirts back and then returns cheerily to his wife with a little spring in his step. The unhappily married man flirts back with purpose and intensity, and tells you that you understand him in a way his wife is incapable of doing. Bit of a circular definition, I know...)

Most importantly, all the spouses need to be comfortable – both mine and my flirtee's. Some people quite enjoy others finding their partner flirt-worthy; after all, if someone is attractive to someone else, he becomes instantly more desirable, right? I know I'm always delighted when a woman flutters her eyelashes at my husband, and he has no problem with me fluttering my own. Nor do I mind when The Architect does his own flirting, though it can be tiresome when he wants to have sex the minute we get home. Some people, however, are very uncomfortable with their partner flirting or being flirted with, and it is vital not to tread on anyone's toes.

There's no doubt whatsoever that flirting can be dangerous, if it gets out of control and leads down the slippery slope towards infidelity. But for most of us, that's about as likely as a piece of chocolate leading to obesity. Generally, it can be taken in moderation and enjoyed, without any harmful side effects.

Of course, flirting is an art form, and it does take some practice. I have learned from bitter experience that the transition from Mum to Flirt can be fraught with difficulties, and that flirting after children can go horribly wrong.

Still, if I can learn, anyone can.

| How to Flirt | How Not to Flirt |
| --- | --- |
| *Playfully pick a piece of fluff off his shirt.* | *Spit on a tissue and wipe food from his mouth.* |
| *Excuse yourself and whisper huskily that you'll be right back.* | *Announce that you need to do a wee-wee.* |
| *Every so often, glance very subtly at his groin.* | *Tell him all the details of your post-partum stitches.* |
| *Display just a hint of cleavage.* | *Say, 'Damn, my boobs are leaking again.'* |

| How to Flirt | How Not to Flirt |
|---|---|
| Admire his pecs and ask if he works out. | Admire his shirt and ask if his wife bought it for him. |
| Ask if his muscles really burn after a hard work-out. | Tell him how unbelievably painful mastitis is. |
| Mention that you work really hard to stay fit and toned. | Mention that you haven't had the time or energy to exercise for three years. |
| Ask him to tell you all about himself. | Talk incessantly about your children. |
| Ask him to tell you all about his work. | Ask him to tell you about his wife's birth experience. |
| Tell him how fascinating his work sounds. | Tell him his work sounds interesting 'but then anything sounds interesting after a day home alone with the baby'. |
| Hint at the wild sex life you enjoy with your partner. | Tell him you've totally gone off sex since giving birth. |
| Give him your full, rapturous attention. | Spend half the conversation making cooing noises at your baby and screaming at your older children. |
| Lean over seductively to show glimpses of your lacy bra. | Lean over clumsily to show glimpses of your maternity bra and breast pads. |
| Tell him his wife is lucky to have such a wonderful man. | Tell him he is lucky to have such a wonderful wife. |
| Twirl strands of your hair around your fingers. | Scratch your head and wonder out loud if you've caught lice from the kids again. |
| Dress to impress. | Have vomit on your top. |
| Wear perfume. | Smell of baby poo and wet wipes. |

| How to Flirt | How Not to Flirt |
| --- | --- |
| *Flutter your eyelids suggestively.* | *Flutter your eyelids closed and fall asleep.* |
| *Tell him you're feeling a bit frisky.* | *Tell him you're ovulating and are hoping for another baby.* |
| *Laugh uproariously at all his jokes.* | *Say, 'Sorry, what? Oh, I didn't get it. I've got baby brain...'* |

# In My Head

There is a great irony when it comes to mothers and sex. We can shy away from the creeping hand of our long-term partner nine nights out of ten but bonk Simon Baker for hours and hours while doing the housework every day. We can see marital sex as a bit of a chore (or a lot of a chore) but think disgracefully inappropriate thoughts about Dr McDreamy, or the barista with the sexy tatts from the cafe down the road.

Of course, this is because there is a vast difference between Fantasy Sex and Real Sex. In Fantasy Sex, you can make love to the man of your dreams, have mind-blowing, endlessly orgasmic intercourse without distractions or inhibitions, and be completely unrestricted by family, fidelity, physical fitness or the laws of physics. In Real Sex, you make love to your husband, whom you have seen naked about a thousand million times, and with whom you are highly unlikely to defy the laws of physics.

You can't keep up crazy passion in a marriage – that adrenaline-pumping, hormone-surging, burning desire that has you swinging from the chandeliers early in the relationship. No matter what the books say, no matter how many new positions you try, no matter what costumes you wear or flavoured oils you sample, you just *can't*.

When you know another person's body like your own, when you live with them, raise kids with them, argue over finances with them, see them sick, wash their socks, and have to remind them to take out the rubbish, you're just not going to tingle every time your hand brushes theirs. And it wouldn't be healthy, anyway. Not only would you have no energy left over for your kids or work, you'd probably die of a heart attack by fifty.

By the time you've had kids and been married for a while, sex is characterised more by an easy familiarity than by any mad, sizzling fervour. Which is fine. Easy familiarity is nice and comforting and can get you where you want to go, if you put in the effort. But it's not crazy passion. And we all need a bit of crazy passion in our lives. Which is where Fantasy Sex comes in.

## Why Fantasy Sex Beats Real Sex

- *In Fantasy Sex, you are not married and you don't have children.*
- *In Fantasy Sex, men like Simon Baker and George Clooney are desperately attracted to you, and shop at your local supermarket, where there is every chance they will bump into you and invite you back to their hotel suite.*
- *In Fantasy Sex, you can have sex on the beach without the discomfort of sand, you can have sex in a forest without the discomfort of foliage, and you can have sex on the floor without any discomfort at all.*
- *In Fantasy Sex, you can change partners mid-session if they're just not doing it for you.*

48

- *In Fantasy Sex, your stretch marks/saggy boobs/haemorrhoids miraculously disappear.*
- *In Fantasy Sex, you are always wearing matching underwear, your legs are always clean-shaven, and your skin is always clear.*
- *In Fantasy Sex, you orgasm just by looking at your partner. And then you orgasm again at will.*
- *In Fantasy Sex, you are the best he's ever had.*
- *In Fantasy Sex, there is no chance of an unwanted pregnancy.*
- *In Fantasy Sex, you never have your period.*
- *In Fantasy Sex, you never get thrush or cystitis.*
- *In Fantasy Sex, you have absolutely no inhibitions (probably because your stretch marks/saggy boobs/haemorrhoids have miraculously disappeared).*
- *In Fantasy Sex, you can smear each other with Nutella without getting all sticky.*
- *You have not seen Fantasy Man do a poo.*
- *Fantasy Man has not seen you push a human being out of your vagina.*
- *You do not share child-rearing duties with Fantasy Man.*
- *You cannot anticipate every sexual move that Fantasy Man will make.*
- *You have not seen Fantasy Man clean his ears and examine the cotton bud for wax.*
- *You have not seen Fantasy Man floss his teeth and examine the floss for foodstuffs.*
- *Fantasy Man is a fantasy. Your husband is family. Family is not sexy.*
- *Fantasy Man will not comment on the fact that you have gained some weight.*
- *Fantasy Man will not comment on your cellulite.*
- *Fantasy Man will not reminisce with you about when your body was younger and more toned.*

➤ *Fantasy Man will not ring you to question you about the credit card bill the morning after.*

➤ *You are not responsible for washing Fantasy Man's underpants.*

➤ *You are not required to be nice to Fantasy Man's mother.*

➤ *You are not required to listen to Fantasy Man clearing his throat at three a.m.*

➤ *You have not seen Fantasy Man's penis several times a day for years.*

➤ *Fantasy Man wakes up with clean, fresh, minty breath.*

➤ *You do not need to argue with Fantasy Man about the household chores, child-rearing or the in-laws. In fact, you do not need to argue with Fantasy Man about anything.*

➤ *Fantasy Man will give you a foot massage. Just because he wants to.*

➤ *Fantasy Man loves to give. He does not need to receive.*

*Love is a Battlefield*

# Women Are from Here, Men Are from Way over There

The Architect and I have very different personalities. I am a show-off. He is shy. I am loud. He is quiet. I am funny. He is actually much funnier, but hey, no one can hear him! I am anxious. He is adventurous. I like shiny shoes. He likes tiny cars. The list goes on and on.

And it's not just our specific characters that are poles apart. Men and women, in general, are different to each other. Men have strange dangly bits which seem to exert a disproportionately large influence on their lives, whereas women's bits are tucked away neatly inside. Men are more left-brained than right, which means that they are more goal-oriented, logical and aggressive, and women are more right-brained than left, which makes us relationship-oriented, emotional and expressive. Men are from Mars, and women are from Venus. We know this. It all makes perfect sense.

Now it's a good thing, really, that we are so different, because most of us wouldn't want to marry a version of ourselves. God knows I wouldn't want to marry someone who needs endless reassurance that he is loved, or who plonks himself on the couch and bursts into tears at the end of a particularly hard day. Nor would I want to hook up with someone who runs around with a pore strip on his nose, or who can be found late at night watching re-runs of *The Mentalist* with his arms up to the elbows in a jar of Nutella. (In fact, thinking about it, I have no idea why The Architect agrees to live with me at all.)

Still, understanding the many theories about why men and women are different doesn't make it any easier to live with a member of the opposite sex. It doesn't hurt any less when you've fallen into the bowl again because your husband has forgotten to put the toilet seat down. It doesn't feel any better when he rolls his eyes dismissively as you tell him about your friend's marital woes. And it doesn't bring much comfort when he informs you matter-of-factly that your bum *does* look big in those new cargo pants. Despite the fact that you asked.

Of course, it's not that women are better than men, or that women are right and men are wrong, at least, not on *every* occasion. It is just that there is a fundamental incompatibility between the sexes that will always persist. It may be overcome by acceptance but it will never, ever change.

## Women Versus Men

🖋 *Women can see. Men, on the other hand, have problems with their sight. Though they may be perfectly able to drive a motor vehicle, read a newspaper, or follow the ball at a cricket match, they simply cannot locate items in the fridge, cupboard or car. In addition, men lack the ability to comprehend that one object may be temporarily hidden behind something else. Women appreciate that objects exist even if they are not immediately visible, yet men believe – no, know – that if an object is not* within their direct line of sight, then it must be lost. And when this happens, it is clearly a man's female partner who did the losing.

🥿 Women can hear. Men, on the other hand, are selectively deaf, or at least become so during the course of a romantic relationship. In the car, travel directions become inaudible, although every word of the sports broadcast can be heard with crystal clarity. In the home, women's voices become inaudible, particularly when they are asking for help around the house. And when taking a nap, everything becomes inaudible, a syndrome which increases exponentially with fatherhood. Though we women can hear our children through two closed doors and industrial-strength earplugs (which we use to block out the sounds of our husbands' throat clearing), men can sleep soundly not only through babies crying, but through kids' birthday parties, toddler tantrums, and visits from the in-laws.

🥿 Women judge men according to their character, intellect, sense of humour, kindness, generosity, warmth, achievements and manners. Men judge women according to whether or not they would have sex with them, and they do so from the moment they are old enough to want to have sex. They do this with every woman they meet, no matter her age, no matter her position. They do it with their friends, their colleagues, your friends, your colleagues, and the partners of their male friends. They do it with your sisters and all of your female relatives. And if your mother is young and attractive enough, they will do it with her, too.

🥿 Women pick up subtleties. Men do not. Hinting to your man that, 'It's almost Valentine's Day!' is about as likely to produce flowers as saying, 'That baby is so cute!' is to result in a pregnancy. Men need things pointed out to them. Not just, 'Valentine's Day is next Monday,' but also, 'It is the day when men are supposed to buy flowers for their partners,' and, 'I want *you to buy some for me. Big, red ones.' On the flip side, men don't actually give hints, either, preferring to be totally direct in their communication (such as, 'I don't believe in Valentine's Day. Get over it'). Of course, if men did communicate in hints, then their female partners would totally get it.*

🗲 *Women enjoy watching their favourite television shows. Men, however, are genetically incapable of watching one television station at a time – unless, of course, an important sporting event is on. In this case, they will remain glued to their seats, screaming at the set, seemingly unaware that their voices do not carry through the screen and into the players' ears. But if they are watching any other programme, especially one in which their female partners are interested (say, for argument's sake, anything with Simon Baker), they will switch the station at every commercial break, causing agonies of uncertainty for their wives, who are painfully aware that they are at constant risk of missing precious minutes of their show.*

🗲 *Women have qualms about being semi-nude in public. Men, generally, do not. They don't agonise over whether they are 'beach-ready' before summer. They do not worry about the roundness of their bellies, they don't baulk at swimwear shopping, and they do not spend hours applying fake tan. When the sun comes out, they happily take off their clothes and bask in its (and their own) glory. And if the opportunity arises for a swim, they will simply strip off and jump right in, pale skin on display for all the world to see. Or is that just my husband? Not even the lack of a swimsuit will deter him; after all, that pair of tattered M&S undies is almost the same thing as Speedos, right? No, darling, wrong, but if I haven't been able to explain this to you after twelve years of marriage and many occasions of humiliation, I don't think I stand a chance now.*

🔖 *Women remember birthdays, anniversaries, term dates, phone numbers, teachers' names, friends' children's names, friends' pets' names, how friends take their coffee, and events important to their loved ones. Men, on the other hand, have selective memories. Oh, they can recall sporting statistics and interest rates with startling accuracy, and the makes and models of cars dating back to the early days of automotive engineering, but they cannot remember birthdays or anniversaries, or the date their mother-in-law is coming to visit.*

🔖 *Women are consistent. Men have double standards. They will criticise women for reading silly magazines and watching mindless television, yet they will devote hours to watching mindless men kick a silly ball around.*

🔖 *Women never rest. Men do. Frequently. Even when the women around them are hard at work cooking, cleaning, and looking after their kids.*

🔖 *Men often believe they are much braver/smarter/more handsome/better in bed/wittier/better dressed and better chefs than they really are. At the same time, they have no idea how brave/smart/beautiful/great in bed/witty/well dressed and what great cooks their female partners are.*

# Ludicrous Debates
## about Preposterous Issues

*M*any couples argue and there is nothing wrong with that at all. In fact, arguing can be highly beneficial. Effective communication is a vital component of any romantic partnership, particularly when it comes to conflict. Couples need to air their disputes with constructive discussion, in order to resolve their issues and develop closer, mutually satisfying relationships.

Which is really my way of justifying that The Architect and I fight all the time.

We have always argued a great deal, without it ever being a problem. Quite the contrary. The occasional big screaming match over who failed to put petrol in the car, who left the milk out overnight or who ruined the other's life is very therapeutic. We yell for a while, bring up everything we've ever done wrong, forgive each other then feel renewed and refreshed. And happily, there are always new things to argue about. After all, it's hard for two people to live together every single day without any kind of conflict, at least not without incurring some kind of severe emotional repression.

Of course, for the most part, the arguments between us are

incredibly repetitive and tiresome. We have the same fights, over and over again, year after year after year, and if they ever do get resolved, or made redundant, they are simply replaced with other, equally repetitive and tiresome fights.

Now, there are exceptions to this rule. The Architect and I have had bizarre, one-off arguments, such as the time we debated whether I'd allow him to travel into space (he said it was his life's ambition; I said it was too dangerous and expensive), or the time he got offended that I hadn't thanked him first in my Golden Globe speech (completely hypothetical, mind you, considering my first and last acting role was in 1984).

However, the majority of our disputes are repeats of arguments we've had approximately 16,000 times before. We fight about tidiness, we fight about money, we fight about his work hours, and we fight about how much I worry. For example, The Architect and I argue endlessly about him not calling to tell me when he's going to be late home. He generally phones me at around seven p.m. to tell me that he's leaving soon, but then gets caught up in a meeting, switches off his phone and rocks up two hours late as if nothing is wrong. Of course, by then I know for a fact that he is dead and am utterly distraught, caught up in visions of myself weeping at his funeral, looking elegant but slightly sexy in a flattering black sheath (not that I would, er, think of my appearance at a time like that). When I confront him tearfully, he rolls his eyes and counters that I'm overanxious, and that I should be used to it by now, seeing as he *always* forgets to tell me when he's running late, and that he hasn't been killed on the job yet (and, being an architect, probably won't, unless he's hit by a flying pen).

But I *don't* get used to it. I *won't* get used to it. So would it be too hard for him to just *call*?

Our other regular argument is about parking fines, which

my husband loves to collect. Every time we receive one of those ominous white envelopes in the post (sent, of course, because The Architect discards the on-the-spot fines that appear on his windscreen), I beg him to be more careful. And every time I beg him to be more careful, he assures me that he has been, that this current fine was from 'a long time ago'. Until the next one arrives. Which also, funnily enough, was from 'a long time ago'. And so it goes on...

We also argue about the boxer shorts on the bathroom floor. Now, The Architect is very diligent about putting all of his dirty clothes into the laundry basket in our bedroom. All, that is, except the boxer shorts in which he sleeps. These, for some unknown, demented reason, he leaves on the bathroom floor.

'Can't you just put your boxers in the basket?' I plead, on a weekly, if not hourly, basis. 'No,' he responds firmly. 'I put everything else in the basket. But I leave my boxers on the floor. Is it such a big deal for you to pick them up?'

It is a ludicrous debate about a preposterous issue, and it will never, ever, ever be resolved. We will be arguing about where he puts his boxer shorts until we are old and grey and have adjoining beds in the nursing home (except by then we won't, of course, because by then the nursing staff will be picking up his boxers, thank God).

Still, I don't mind fighting. At times, I even enjoy it. Or at least I did, until the kids came along.

And then, as with every other aspect of our lives, everything changed.

# Not in Front of the Kids

*D*espite our lust (and aptitude) for fighting, the rules of engagement changed once we had children. And, suddenly, fighting was much less fun.

You see, once children are born, adults simply aren't meant to argue anymore. Families are supposed to be havens of love and security, which means that we parents have to be nice to each other in front of our offspring. In other words, we have to do all of our fighting when the kids aren't around.

But here's the catch. The kids are always around.

So we have to present a united front. Well, being united as a couple is hard enough at the best of times. As you know, The Architect and I have many areas of disagreement. But when we became parents, these areas were multiplied, because having kids gave us so much more to argue about. Not only do I have to deal with all of The Architect's regular crazy-making habits, oh no, I now must contend with the new and maddening sphere of his poor child-raising practices.

So no longer do I just get upset when my husband comes home late at night. Now I get upset when my husband comes home late at night and gets the children out of bed to play with them an hour after their bedtime. And as it is unacceptable to yell at my husband in front of the kids, I have to squeak out a tortured, 'Wow, a late-night family pillow-fight. How very nice.'

And herein lies the crux of all parental conflict: the kids give you issues to fight about, but you can't fight about issues in front of the kids. It's very frustrating.

You can always try postponing the argument until later. But scheduled fights don't work very well for me. It's kind of like scheduling sex. You make a date for when the kids are in bed, but when the time finally comes around, you've forgotten what got you all hot and bothered in the first place and you just want to go to sleep.

Of course, you still have the option of the post-argument walkout. Whoever is the most incensed at the end of the argument announces, 'That's it! I'm leaving!', and storms self-righteously out of the house. When you don't have any kids, walking out makes you the loser. You have to leave the house with nowhere particular to go, while your spouse gets to remain at home with the television, the bed, and the fridge full of food. When you're a parent, however, this situation is completely reversed. Walking out makes you the winner – you get to leave the house with nowhere particular to go, while your partner has to remain at home with the laundry, the mess, and three hyped-up kids.

So there is still the potential for a satisfying resolution to a parental conflict. There's the possibility of gaining an hour or so of free time, maybe dropping in on a friend, even grabbing a cappuccino. I just have to beat my husband to the door.

Of course, I don't always beat my husband to the door, and I do recognise that screaming matches and storm-outs aren't necessarily productive. Or mature.

So with this in mind, I have developed a process. It's for use by couples experiencing issues in their relationship and follows the road bravely forged by human resources professionals over the past century.

You fill out a form.

The form has a list of options, and boxes to tick, and will efficiently file complaints into clear categories for easy future reference. I believe it will do wonders for the speedy resolution of marital discord situations, promoting domestic harmony and familial contentment. And it will save a hell of a lot of useless talking.

The Marital Complaint Form
*Name of Complainant:* ..................................................
*Name of Offending Spouse:* ...........................................
*Cause of Complaint (please tick as many as applicable):*
❑ Late home from work.
❑ Late home from pub.
❑ Late home from other *(please specify):* ...................
❑ Was rude to me.
❑ Was rude to my friends.
❑ Was rude to other *(please specify):* ......................
❑ Forgot birthday.
❑ Forgot anniversary.
❑ Forgot bread and milk.
❑ Forgot other *(please specify):* ...........................
❑ Left dirty clothes on floor.
❑ Left dirty dishes on table.
❑ Sided with mother over me.
❑ Too demanding.
❑ Asks me for sex all the time.
❑ Never wants to have sex.
❑ Too hard on the kids.
❑ Too easy on the kids.
❑ Gets the kids hyped up before bed.
❑ Told me my bum looked big.
❑ Failed to tell me how big my bum looked.
❑ Other *(please specify):* ..................................
❑ I don't need to have a reason!
*Signature of Complainant:* ...........................................
*Resolution of Offending Spouse to Do Better in Future:*

..........................................................................

# Part Two: Them

## Becoming Mum

# I Caught Vomit in My Hands

Technically, you become a mother at the moment you give birth, or when you're handed your adoptive baby. This, however, isn't necessarily the point at which you start feeling like a mother. I certainly didn't feel like a parent the second I held my first baby. I was fascinated by him – this huge-eyed mini-Architect baby – but I was equally as fascinated by the fact that my legs were completely numb after having had an epidural. ('Wow. Check it out! I can stick needles into them and I can't feel a thing!')

When I first took Little Man out in his pram I felt inordinately proud of my baby, but also strangely fraudulent. I was sure that anyone looking closely would recognise that I was only playing at being a mum, and that I had absolutely no idea what I was doing. I also suspected that if they peered into the pram they would see that I wasn't pushing around a baby at all but a dolly – albeit one who looked remarkably like my husband, only with a freakishly large head.

Still, at some point in my son's life I did begin to feel like his mother. One minute I was staring at this big-headed crying stranger, wondering how on earth he came to be there, and the next minute I was picking him up and cradling him in my arms, knowing that I was the only one who could soothe him and give him exactly what he needed. And I realised it had happened. I was a mum.

The dawning of motherhood occurs differently for everyone. It can happen the first time you gaze into your newborn's eyes. It can happen the first time you manage to soothe your baby when no one else can. It can happen the first minute your baby successfully latches on to your breast without you clenching your teeth in agony. Or it can happen the first time you see your baby cradled in the arms of an unappealing relative, and you feel an overpowering, instinctive desire to snatch him out of her fetid hands and return him to the safety of your own warm embrace. (Or perhaps that just happened to me.)

Over the following months and years you find yourself doing things you never would have dreamed of doing – things you never imagined would be the logical progression of growing a human being in your womb. Because motherhood doesn't just come with a new set of skills. It fundamentally changes the person you are.

## I Knew I Was a Mother When...

- ♀ *I didn't think twice about eating food off the floor.*
- ♀ *I didn't think twice about eating food from someone else's plate.*
- ♀ *I didn't think twice about eating food from someone else's mouth.*
- ♀ *I began secreting cleaning fluid in my saliva which could remove anything from my child's face (well, not literally, but I acted like I did).*

♀ *I didn't notice when someone was fiddling with my breasts in public (it was my child, but it pretty much could have been anybody).*

♀ *I didn't notice when my child was watching me on the toilet (in fact, I didn't notice when someone else's child was watching me on the toilet).*

♀ *I thought nothing of sticking my hand down a nappy to check for poo (until one day, the hand came out with poo on it, at which point I deeply regretted my actions).*

♀ *I caught vomit in my hands – and not just my own vomit.*

♀ *I noticed vomit on my shirt when I was out in public.*

♀ *I noticed vomit on my shirt when I was out in public and brushed it off with my bare hands.*

♀ *I noticed vomit on my shirt when I was out in public and didn't bother brushing it off at all.*

♀ *I discovered my handbag contained a nappy, a month-old Vegemite sandwich, three snotty tissues, and the headless torso of a Barbie doll.*

♀ *I found myself mindlessly rocking the cot even though the baby was downstairs with The Architect.*

♀ *I went shopping for jeans for myself and came home with two adorable Babygros, a pair of kiddie sunglasses, and a small polka-dot giraffe.*

♀ *I bit someone else's fingernails.*

♀ *I removed someone else's snot.*

♀ *I began fantasising about sleep like I used to fantasise about chocolate and sex (although I still regularly fantasised about chocolate).*

♀ *I considered seven a.m. to be a 'sleep-in'.*

♀ *I considered nine p.m. to be a 'late night'.*

♀ *I knew every delousing technique known to humankind.*

♀ *I knew the quickest route to the children's hospital.*

♀ *I knew the best parking spots near the children's hospital.*

♀ I stopped fantasising about jewellery and clothes and started fantasising about having a full-time nanny.

♀ I stopped rating my friend's husbands on their attractiveness, intelligence and sense of humour, and started rating them on how much they helped out with their kids.

♀ I guarded my babysitter's details with my life.

♀ I found myself lingering in the aisles of Waitrose just appreciating the wonder of being alone.

♀ The baby health nurse recognised my voice on the phone.

♀ My GP's receptionist recognised my voice on the phone.

♀ The Poisons Information Line operator recognised my voice on the phone.

# One Day You Will
# Cut Your Child's Hair

*W*e all know birth is going to hurt, although happily, we can't possibly anticipate how much. This is because, no matter how much we think we are prepared, we cannot actually feel something we have not yet experienced. The same is true of falling in love. The same is true of grief.

And the same is true of motherhood.

We can read all the books in the world about babies, we can do prenatal courses, we can talk to our parents about their experiences, and cuddle every baby of every friend we've ever had, but we still cannot imagine what it will feel like to look down at our own child whom we created. We cannot anticipate the smell of its head or the softness of its tummy or the wrenching pull of its cry. We cannot understand what it feels like to be responsible for another human being twenty-four hours a day, every single day, for the rest of our lives. We can read books about toddlers, and raising boys, and raising girls, and parenting, and happy families, and ADHD, and gifted children, but nothing – *nothing* – can prepare us for the multitude of tasks and negotiations and emotions and frustrations that constitute parenting. These are things we just have to find out for ourselves, as we stumble along the way.

We can decide that we're going to be earth mothers, attachment parents, that our kids won't watch TV, that they'll only eat organic food, that we'll have a strict routine, that we'll be completely flexible, that we'll stay home with them for five years, that we'll go back to work a month after they are born, that we'll have only one child, two kids, three kids, a dozen... And then our first baby is born and all our firm intentions go out the window and we are left with the stark reality of getting to know a person we have created, but about whom we know absolutely nothing. And then some things – and sometimes everything – can change.

It is a truth universally acknowledged that we will love our babies, with time, anyway. It is a truth universally acknowledged that motherhood is hard. We know that. We expect that. But there are other truths that we cannot foresee, until we find ourselves at nine-fifteen p.m., outside in the freezing cold in our dressing-gown, searching through the rubbish bin for our son's lost merit award as he watches, distraught, from the window, and we realise, 'Right. So *this* is what it's all about.'

## Things They Don't Tell You about Motherhood

- At some point in the future, the gorgeous baby to whom you gave birth with pain, who you fed, nurtured, protected, and loved, will turn around and tell you that you're a big, stupid idiot.

- Your child will have friends whom you despise, because they're whiny, loud, disrespectful, annoying, or simply have unspeakably irritating faces. And you'll still be forced to have these friends over for play dates, feeding them and supervising them *through clenched teeth, while all the time fantasising about locking them in a dark cupboard. And they haven't even reached infants school.*

- *Your child will have friends whose parents you despise, and you will be forced to have them over for cups of tea and discussions about their bratty children, while all the time fantasising about locking them in a dark cupboard.*

- *Your child will never be on stage for more than one minute in the average school concert.*

- *The average school concert will last for two hours.*

- *The average school concert will feel like it lasts for six hours.*

- *You will film one hour and fifty-nine minutes of the school concert. You will miss the one minute of your child's appearance.*

- *You will tape footage of your knee over important videos of your child.*

- *It takes approximately an hour and a half to buy school shoes when you leave it until the day before school starts.*

- *You will leave buying shoes until the day before school starts.*

- *The behaviour of your children will be in inverse proportion to the importance of your need to impress the people you are with. When you're out with your best friend and her unruly kids, your kids will be angelic. When you're out with your sister-in-law and her perfect children, your kids will be little devils.*

- *Your child will look ridiculous in every single school photo, yet you will pay an exorbitant sum of money for the prints.*

- *At some stage in your child's life, you will attempt to cut their hair. Unless you are a hairdresser, this will make your child look like a demented escapee from the Starship Enterprise.*

- *The clothes your daughter looks most beautiful in will lie dormant at the bottom of her wardrobe. She will wear her 'I'm a hot sexy chicken' T-shirt until you peel it from her sleeping body.*

- *Your child will unexpectedly lose a tooth late at night and the tooth fairy will need to leave an IOU.*
- *You will pay lots of money for a relaxing holiday at a resort with a kids' club. Your children will refuse to go to the kids' club.*
- *You will maim your child at some point, either by buckling their tummy into the car seat, jamming their fingers in the highchair, burning them accidentally with your hair straightener (don't ask), or by innumerable other methods. Your child will recover within minutes. You will be scarred for life.*
- *Covering books in contact paper is ridiculously difficult, time-consuming and boring. You will be required to do it every year, over and over again, for a long, long, long time.*
- *Your children will generate more laundry than you ever thought possible.*
- *Your child will exchange the fifty-pound Nintendo game you bought him for a friend's one-pound Mighty Beanz bean because he 'really loves Mighty Beanz' and 'the game is boring'.*
- *When dining out, no matter how many times you ask the waitress, the kids' meals will come twenty minutes after your meal, so that no one enjoys their food.*
- *Your toddler will need to urgently wee at the most inconvenient moment possible. When a toilet is in easy reach, she'll stay dry all day.*

## Make Him Drink the Bathwater

*H*aving your first baby is always going to be a massive shock to the system. Come to think of it, having any new baby is going to be a massive shock to the system, as introducing a new human being into the world generally is.

Still, there are ways you can make the transition to motherhood easier.

Books are useful, but they don't give you hands-on experience. Looking after other people's kids does give you hands-on experience, but you can still hand the children back at the end of the day, and, quite frankly, what is motherhood without the endless, unrelenting permanence of the situation?

I'd read several books before Little Man was born and they were very helpful. They told me everything I needed to know about pureeing vegetables, changing nappies and caring for my nipples. Unfortunately, however, they told me nothing about managing the huge changes to my life that children would bring: the shift in focus, the small frustrations, the sleep deprivation, and the daunting, relentless sense of responsibility.

Still, I wasn't completely clueless, or at least, I wasn't as clueless as some. One woman I know – the first in her circle to give birth – actually asked her midwife how she should brush her baby's teeth, so completely naive was she about babies (and their mouths). I'd babysat as a teenager, and knew that babies didn't have teeth. Even so, my experience of playing with children for an hour before bedtime didn't prepare me in the slightest for living with them twenty-four hours a day.

The only way to prepare yourself for motherhood, the only way to gain meaningful training, is to simulate the experience for an extended period of time. This way, when the actual baby arrives, you will have some realistic appreciation of how your life will change forever.

So how do you do this? Well, I have devised a simple programme. It requires your partner (or, in the absence of a partner, a friend) to adopt some of the behaviours that you are likely to encounter when you have a child. This will allow you to prepare yourself for the role of parent, and to begin perfecting some strategies for dealing with it.

## *The Motherhood Preparation Programme*

Your partner must:

- *Eat with his fingers.*
- *Fling bits of his dinner in your face.*
- *Reply 'I don't know' or 'Chocolate' when asked what he wants to eat.*
- *Reply 'I don't know' or 'Stupid head' when asked his name.*
- *Reply, 'I don't know' or 'You're a stupid head' when asked how his day was.*
- *Plonk himself down in the supermarket and refuse to budge until you have given him a treat.*
- *Yell, 'No!' for no apparent reason at random intervals during the day.*
- *Run around the house with his underwear on his head.*
- *Remove his clothing at every opportunity.*

- Loudly inform you whenever his private parts are itchy.
- Loudly inform you whenever he needs to do a poo.
- Loudly inform complete strangers whenever he has done a poo.
- Loudly interrupt you whenever you are doing a poo.
- Interrupt sex by crying and saying that he's had a bad dream.
- Insist on being carried.
- Refuse to go to bed.
- Refuse to get out of bed.
- Empty the Tupperware cupboard.
- Draw on the walls with marker pen.
- Draw on himself with marker pen.
- Suck on the end of a marker pen until his entire mouth is bright green.
- Smear his entire body and hair with Nutella.
- Attempt to cuddle you while smeared from head to toe in Nutella.
- Cling to you and cry whenever you leave the house.
- Smack his siblings and friends whenever your back is turned.
- Say he didn't do it.
- Beg you to make pancakes.
- Say, 'Yuck, I hate pancakes,' when pancakes are served.
- Yell, 'I want to stay home!' when it's time to go out.
- Yell, 'I don't want to go home!' when it's time to go home.
- Vomit after consuming his own body weight in junk food at a party.
- Play I-spy with you and spy things he can't actually see.
- Drink the bathwater.
- Answer the phone by yelling, 'Hellooooo!' then drop the phone and run away.
- Ask where babies come from.
- Ask what God looks like.
- Tell you you're mean and horrible.
- Tell you you're beautiful and that he loves you more than anything in the whole wide world.

# When One Is Not Enough

*M*otherhood is difficult. (I believe I may have mentioned that before, but it cannot be reiterated frequently enough.) And yet, many of us aren't satisfied to be a mother once. Instead, we do it again, and often again and again, having two kids, or three (in my case), even four or five or (and I'm struggling to retain empathy for this one) six or more children. Why?

Well, obviously we love our kids and want to spread the love. What's more, we have ideas in our head about the size of the family we want to create, and many of us are lucky enough to make that idea a reality.

When Little Man was born, I always thought of him as my first child. I knew that – sooner rather than later – I would try to fall pregnant again, hopefully this time with a girl. (Now for the record, I *know* that this is a politically incorrect thing to say. I *know* that all I was supposed to care about was the health of my baby, not its gender. But the truth is that I had always longed for a little girl. I know I would have madly loved any child who arrived, but when my Pinkela arrived with a shiny, as she would later call it, I was absolutely beside myself.)

Still, how did I get over the agony of childbirth and decide to do it all again? The conventional wisdom is that we forget the pain – or at least how really, really, *really* bad it is. I disagree. I can still close my eyes and recall every minute of my labours. But somehow I got past it. I put it into a compartment in my mind labelled 'Most Painful Thing Ever', and moved on to the nappies and laundry.

But it wasn't just the pain of childbirth that should have formed a disincentive. What happened after I got through the challenges of the first year – no sleep, sore nipples, flabby stomach, dirty nappies, vomit, pureed veggies, and did I mention no sleep? – to convince me, 'That was fun! Let's do it again!'? What happened after I nearly lost my mind looking after a toddler and a newborn to make me decide, 'They're both at school now; why not start at the very beginning again and have another?'

Well, a few things, really.

## Why I Went Again

- *I thought that the biggest change to our lives was having our first child. I was wrong. Having Pinkela doubled the work. And having Toddler pretty much quadrupled it.*

- *I thought that after experiencing the tortures of sleep deprivation the first time I would cope with it much better the second time around. I didn't. I found it harder. Instead of waking in the middle of the night and sighing, I would wake up in the middle of the night and sob. Often louder than the baby.*

- *I thought I would get the breastfeeding/teaching to sleep/toilet training thing right this time. Well, I did get it, but my new baby didn't at all.*

- *I thought that after the challenging baby I had first time around I'd get a gentle, easy little girl the next time. And guess what? I did! Pinkela was the sweet, good-natured, smiley child I had always* dreamed of. And then I had another baby. And I got Toddler. Loud, cheery, hilarious, mad-as-a-cut-snake Toddler. Sigh.

- I thought I would know what I was doing the next time, and that I would approach parenting with the confidence, assurance and knowledge born of experience. Wrong. I realise now that I could bear seventeen children and still have no idea what to do when they lie screaming on the floor in the supermarket.

- I thought that it would be fun and enriching for my son to have a playmate. When we brought Pinkela home from the hospital, Little Man tried to put her into the bin.

- I thought kids were adaptable, and that my son would get used to having a younger sibling in no time. Nine years later he is still complaining about how unfair it is that he has to share.

- I thought a bigger family would be warmer, more loving, more nurturing, and ... well ... more family-like. And it is. It is a joy. I still get a thrill from looking at my three children and thinking, 'Oh! I made them all!' My big family is beautiful. It is also noisier, chaotic, more expensive, and harder to transport.

- I thought that the big kids would help me with the baby. And they do. If feeding her chocolate biscuits, teaching her how to say 'pooey bum bum', and making her carry their backpacks can be considered 'helping'.

- I thought that Pinkela and Toddler would live on hand-me-downs and recycled toys. But they don't. Their sibling's clothes have always been the wrong season, the toys were always for the wrong gender, and Little Man has destroyed most of them, anyway.

- I thought my body had been stretched to the max after my first pregnancy, and that I really couldn't look any worse. I was wrong. Oh, how wrong I was.

# Don't Believe What You See

*I* don't watch soap operas. I don't have time. And if I did have a few minutes to turn on the TV during the day, I'd watch a news broadcast, or a re-run of something with Simon Baker.

A few years back, however, I was struck down with hepatitic glandular fever (which is much like regular glandular fever, except that you feel even worse, and turn a funny shade of yellow) and I was forced to spend several weeks recuperating in bed, a time I now look back upon as a hallowed period of rest.

During these weeks of my recovery I watched a great deal of daytime television. While many of the soap operas depicted glamorous young women without children, many of them also depicted glamorous young women with children. Even in my weakened state I was struck by how outrageously different the lives of these soap opera mothers were to my life, and to the lives of pretty much every mother I have ever met.

So if you don't have any kids, please don't believe what you see on daytime TV. I can assure you, it's not like that at all. Though frequently, I really, *really* wish it was...

## Soap Opera Mum? Not Me

♀ *Soap opera mothers wake up in the morning in full make-up. I rarely find time to apply make-up, and if I do, I virtually never have the time to remove it. By the end of the day, the only thing I want to do is sleep, not start cleansing and toning. So if there is any make-up to be found in bed in the morning, it is most likely to be on my pillow.*

♀ *Soap opera mothers sleep between satin sheets. I sleep between frayed sheets that have been scribbled on with marker pen.*

♀ *Soap opera mothers sip tea from elegant china cups. I drink coffee that has been going cold on the kitchen counter for half an hour. In a cracked mug.*

♀ *Soap opera mothers never seem to eat. I eat. A lot. And often with my fingers.*

♀ *Soap opera mothers have pregnancy-free babies. I got really fat for about twelve months. Three times.*

♀ *Soap opera mothers have children who are very quiet, beautifully dressed, and impeccably groomed. I have kids who are very noisy, often naked, and have bits of yesterday's frankfurter in their hair.*

♀ *Soap opera mothers have really long fingernails. If I had really long fingernails, I would scratch my children or get Unspeakable Sticky Stuff under my nails.*

♀ *Soap opera mothers have sleek, smooth hair at all times, even first thing in the morning or when waking from a two-year coma. I have about as much time to make my hair sleek and smooth as I do to apply make-up. Or to wipe it off.*

♀ *Soap opera mothers have servants who wear starched uniforms. I have a cleaning lady once a week, and I have to tidy up for her before she arrives.*

♀ *Soap opera mothers say things like, 'Guthrie, would you please fetch the limousine?' I say things like, 'Where the hell are my keys?' and 'Don't rub banana into the seat.'*

♀ *Soap opera mothers travel on private jets owned by their fabulously wealthy lovers. I travel on low-fare airlines with tickets I booked on the internet.*

♀ *Soap opera mothers have deep, dark secrets. I feel compelled to tell my friends when my bra is uncomfortable.*

♀ *Soap opera mothers discover long-lost, evil twin sisters. I find it hard to find my keys, let alone amnesiac missing persons.*

♀ *Soap opera mothers marry every man they know at least once. I'm just not that interested in sex.*

♀ *Soap opera mothers have silk robes, which they wear with fluffy high-heeled mules. I have a pink dressing-gown, given to me on my birthday, which I team with The Architect's old socks.*

♀ *Soap opera mothers have sex very rarely, but when they do they remain discreetly covered. Well, at least the first part of that statement is true for me...*

♀ *Soap opera mothers have discussions with their back to the person they're conversing with, so that both of them can be facing the camera at once. I don't do that. For a start, there's no camera. For another thing, it's just stupid.*

♀ *Soap opera mothers punctuate their conversations with meaningful looks into midair. I'd do that, but my kids never let me finish a train of thought.*

♀ *Soap opera women get amnesia. I had baby brain, but that's about it.*

♀ *Soap opera mothers engage in long-term feuds with powerful adversaries from rival dynasties. I engage in short-term feuds with very small adversaries who call me Mum.*

♀ *Soap opera mothers never go outdoors. I do. Have you ever tried staying home all day with a toddler?*

# People I Grew in My Womb

## Save for Therapy

*P*regnancy can be a very anxious time. When I was pregnant with Little Man I worried about all sorts of things. I worried that I'd drown my baby in the bath, for no apparent reason other than that I'd heard of it happening. I worried that I'd forget how to assemble the pram at a crucial moment, and that we would find ourselves stranded in public with a whole lot of groceries and no means of getting home. I worried about becoming too emotionally involved with my child, too smothering and overprotective. And, most of all, I worried about being too worried – about being such an anxious parent that I'd turn my child into a neurotic mess.

Of course, like everyone else, I've just done my best at this mothering gig, and have so far managed to muddle through without inflicting any (major) permanent injury or (debilitating) psychological damage on my three children – although to be fair, the extent of any damage will not be truly apparent for another ten or twenty years. I've certainly stuffed up on about 25,000 occasions, but it has never been in the ways I'd anticipated.

I never drowned any of my children in the bath. I did,

however, manage to allow Pinkela to slip off a pier into freezing water in the middle of winter when she was about two. She was walking between The Architect and me and literally catapulted herself into the river, sinking before our eyes. There was just enough time for me to look at my husband and say, 'You get her,' and for him to throw off his jacket and jump in. She was fine, but the memory haunted me for years. Still does, really.

I worked out how to assemble the pram very quickly (okay, very slowly, after hours of prenatal practice with the role of the baby being played by a teddy bear). And yet, though I never got caught with a collapsed pram, I did once get caught with a collapsed baby, after forgetting to strap Little Man into his stroller and tipping him out onto the floor.

I vigorously fought the tendency to become an overanxious parent. Then, as it turns out, I became so resolutely laid back that I ignored a growing rash on Pinkela's torso (a complication from chicken pox) until she was rushed to the hospital in toxic shock. She recovered after ten days on a drip. I'm still recovering from that one.

And, of course, after worrying that I would be overprotective and smothering, I have ended up racked with guilt that as a working mother I don't spend enough quality time with my kids.

You can never win. Or at least, I can't.

The reality is that all mothers are fallible, simply because all people are fallible. Giving birth doesn't automatically give you parenting skills. Having children doesn't make you understand your kids. And being a mother doesn't stop you from making mistakes.

It just makes you feel really guilty about them.

# You Need to Start a Therapy Fund for Your Child When...

- They see you sobbing with greater gusto than they ever could.
- They see you curled up in the foetal position on the couch.
- They catch you and your partner bitterly arguing.
- They catch you and your partner passionately making up.
- They find one of those special 'marriage spicing' toys you ordered from the internet.
- They catch you slurring your words and giggling with a bottle of 'grown-up juice' in your hand.
- They catch you stark naked with a hair colourant on your head and a pore strip on your nose as you pluck grey hairs from your bikini area.
- They find you in the shower wearing a tampon, and ask why you have 'a string in your bum'.
- They ask you what sex is then sob with fear when you tell them.
- They enter the house bleeding from an injury and you scream in panic and run from the room.
- You yell at them for being badly behaved before realising they have fever of forty-one degrees.
- You yell at them for not drinking their milk before realising it is three days past the expiry date.
- You yell at them for losing their shoes before realising you have put them in your closet.
- You forget to pick them up from school and find them sitting in agitation next to an annoyed teacher.
- You forget to pick them up from a party and find them sitting in agitation next to an annoyed parent.
- You drop them at school in full uniform on a mufti day and find them dejected and shamed at pick-up time.
- You forget to pack a bear for Special Toys Day and leave them sobbing at the school gate in despair.

🍼 You yell at them for no particular reason other than that you're premenstrual and exhausted. Saying something reasonably innocuous like, 'You kids drain my will to live.'

# *You Need to Start a Therapy Fund for Yourself When...*

🔖 You collapse your pram with the baby still inside as your older child looks on in horror.

🔖 You unpack your shopping from the car but forget to unpack your sleeping toddler. You only remember that you left your sleeping toddler in the car when your mother calls an hour later to ask how the little one is.

🔖 You watch as the only bottle of formula you have rolls out of your bag and onto the road and gets run over by a truck.

🔖 You lose your child in the supermarket.

🔖 You lose your child at the beach.

🔖 You lose your child at home.

🔖 You find your child sitting on a stranger's lap, eating a bag of suspicious-looking lollies.

🔖 You accidentally snip off the top of your baby's finger when trying to trim their nails.

🔖 You realise you've been using the television as a babysitter. For fourteen hours straight.

🔖 You smack your child in anger, having always promised yourself you would never, ever smack your child in anger (though you are still not sure why you would smack your child if you weren't angry).

🔖 You find yourself longing for a glass of wine at six o'clock every evening. Five o'clock. Four o'clock. Three o'clock. Two o'clock...

# Endless Chatter

*K*ids come in different shapes and sizes (although all generally begin as 'small') and have different personalities. Some
kids are introverted, some are extroverted, some are cheeky,
some are kind, some are moody, some are peaceable, some are
wild, and some are serene. But nearly all, in my experience,
love to talk. My three kids are as different from each other as
frankfurters are from mashed potatoes. However, all three are
incessant talkers (although admittedly Toddler's conversation
can be somewhat garbled at this point). Endless talking is a
special trait of the younger child. While teenagers are known
for being withdrawn and grunty, young kids want to share
every detail of their life with you, from what level they reached
on their Nintendo game to when they last did a poo.

Of course, each child has his or her own special interest.
Little Man can describe his day at school in excruciatingly – I
mean, fascinatingly – minute detail. I will pick him up from
school and during the twenty-minute drive home we will cover
only the first two hours of his day, with the other remaining
four hours still to be recounted. Pinkela, on the other hand,
is less forthcoming about school, but will relate the plot of a
movie in more time than it would take to watch the film itself,
or a book with further detail than was originally written. Her

enthusiasm delights me for the first three minutes, bores me for the following three minutes, irritates me for the next ten, and has me fantasising about stabbing myself in the eye from then on.

In addition to enjoying hearing themselves talk (or, in Toddler's case, sing loudly and with no particular tune), my kids also like to ask a great deal of questions. Many times they wish to know the answers to particular burning concerns; at other times, they simply use questions as convenient grammatical constructions to allow them to further hear their own voices. Toddler, for example, will invariably announce: 'Mum, I have a question!'

'What, darling?' I will ask.

'Blue!' she will say.

Kids also get fixated on particular issues at different times. Little Man went through an extreme weather phase, during which he gleefully enquired about the consequences of various catastrophic meteorological disasters, from floods to hurricanes to heatwaves. Pinkela, on the other hand, is more concerned about issues of career and of the heart. She asks frequent questions about what she should be when she grows up and who she should marry, with greater urgency and anxiety than one might expect from a person of nine years.

Toddler, on the other hand, generally just asks for chocolate. But often.

## Questions Kids Ask

- 🐸 *Where is God?*
- 🐸 *What does God look like?*
- 🐸 *What happens after you die?*
- 🐸 *When will you die?*

When will I die?

Why do people have to die?

Why are people so mean?

What is sex?

Why do people do sex?

Why do people do sex if they don't want a baby?

Do you do sex with Daddy?

Can I watch you do sex?

Why can't I watch you do sex?

Do I ever have to do sex?

Why is my penis so hard?

Why don't I have a penis?

Why is the sky blue?

Why can't I go for a walk by myself?

Why can't I stay home by myself?

What will happen if our house burns down?

What will happen if a meteor crashes into earth?

What will happen if a hurricane hits us?

Why did you say Tim's mum is a silly cow?

Why does that man have no hair?

Why does that man have no legs?

Why does that man have no chin?

Are black people born white and turn black slowly?

Why do I have to go to school?

Why do I have to do homework?

What is gay?

How do gay people make a baby?

How can people have a baby when they're not married?

What does alcohol do?

What do drugs do?

Why do people have drugs?

Have you ever had drugs?

# In One Ear, Out the Other

We all know what mums are *supposed* to say. All we have to do is pick up a parenting book to be bombarded with the messages of positive reinforcement we should be giving our kids every day. You know, phrases like, 'Way to go!', 'You're a star!' or, 'I'm so proud of you!' Uplifting words, it is true, but it can be tough to heap praise on a child when all they have done on a particular day is stuff Weetabix into the DVD player, drink the bathwater, and tell the lady at the check-out that she has a funny nose. Still, these are the things we are supposed to say. 'I love you.' 'You're the best.' 'You're doing so well.'

But these are words for an ideal world, in which kids are endlessly praiseworthy, and we mothers are constantly appreciative. And the real world, as we know, is not ideal. In the real world, kids are intermittently praiseworthy, in between long stretches of complaining about homework, refusing to eat their vegetables, and calling each other 'Smelly Bum Bum'. So what do we mothers really say? What are the words that actually come out of our mouths, day after day, hour after hour, innumerable times over the course of our parenting lives?

## *What Mums Say*

- ⅃ *In a minute.*
- ⅃ *Just a sec.*
- ⅃ *Hang on.*
- ⅃ *What?*
- ⅃ *What NOW?*
- ⅃ *No!*
- ⅃ *Wait.*
- ⅃ *Not yet.*
- ⅃ *Later!*
- ⅃ *When I say so.*
- ⅃ *If you behave.*
- ⅃ *Only if you behave.*
- ⅃ *Can't you just behave?*
- ⅃ *BEHAVE!*
- ⅃ *There's going to be SUCH TROUBLE if you don't behave!*
- ⅃ *Eat your dinner.*
- ⅃ *Eat some of your dinner.*
- ⅃ *Eat three mouthfuls.*
- ⅃ *Just eat two mouthfuls.*
- ⅃ *Okay, one more mouthful.*
- ⅃ *Fine, don't eat. See if I care.*
- ⅃ *Don't you dare be rude!*
- ⅃ *Don't you dare hit me!*
- ⅃ *Don't you dare do that again!*
- ⅃ *Don't. You. Dare.*
- ⅃ *Did you just do what I think you did?*
- ⅃ *Who started it?*
- ⅃ *Who hit who?*
- ⅃ *Why did you hit him?*
- ⅃ *Apologise.*

🥿 *Apologise RIGHT NOW.*

🥿 *There's going to be SUCH TROUBLE if you don't apologise!*

🥿 *I'll know if you're not telling the truth.*

🥿 *Don't you lie to me.*

🥿 *One.*

🥿 *Only one!*

🥿 *NOW!*

🥿 *RIGHT NOW, young lady.*

🥿 *Because I said so.*

🥿 *Just because!*

🥿 *I don't have to give you a reason.*

🥿 *Stop that noise.*

🥿 *Stop fighting.*

🥿 *Just. Stop.*

🥿 *Why do you never know when to stop?*

🥿 *There's going to be SUCH TROUBLE if you don't stop!*

🥿 *Be quiet.*

🥿 *Enough!*

🥿 *No more!*

🥿 *Not again!*

🥿 *When are you going to learn?*

🥿 *What were you thinking?*

🥿 *I'm very disappointed in you.*

🥿 *I'm very angry at you.*

🥿 *Fine. I forgive you.*

🥿 *Just this once.*

🥿 *Last chance.*

🥿 *No more chances.*

🥿 *Okay, one more chance.*

🥿 *Yes, I still love you.*

🥿 *Of course I love you.*

🥿 *I love you, too.*

🥿 *I love you more than anything in the world.*

# Maternal Creative Truths

*A* lot of words come out of a mother's mouth every day. Many of these words are directive or forceful. Many of these words are loving, or compassionate, or supportive.

But many of these words ... well ... they are not 100 per cent genuine, totally honest, truths.

Now, it's not that we mothers lie, per se. As we do with our husbands, we just extend the truth on occasion. After all, a mother without a little white lie is like a fighter pilot without a parachute. You hope you won't need to use one, but if the situation calls for it and you don't have one handy, you're going to crash and burn.

So yes, I tell the occasional Maternal Creative Truth. When particularly tired, I might agree with Pinkela that the minuscule scratch on her leg is very serious, and that she can't possibly be allowed to go to her swimming lesson. I will also earnestly explain the same to the swimming teacher the following week, in the hope of being granted a make-up lesson, which we will not attend anyway as we can't be bothered.

I will pretend to the cashier that I have no idea how Toddler got her hands on that half-eaten Kinder Surprise, when five minutes earlier I distinctly heard her say, 'Mama, I go get chocky!'

I tell Toddler that the lollies in the pharmacy are medicine and that she won't like them. This can cause confusion when she sees Daddy eating jelly beans. 'What wrong, Daddy? You eat medicine! You sick?'

I tell my mother that I am extremely strict about what my children watch on TV. And I am. They are not allowed to watch pornography, or anything at all with Nigella Lawson in it.

I set Little Man's bedside clock a bit early, so that when he wakes at six-thirty (the time he's allowed to rise) he thinks it's only six-twenty and stays in bed for an extra ten minutes. And in case you're wondering, this doesn't make me feel guilty. It makes me feel more rested.

I lie about the reasons I am late. I blame Little Man (lost his shoes, left his homework inside, last-minute poo), Pinkela (lost her hair brush, fell over walking out the door, last-minute poo) or Toddler (hid my keys, spilt her juice all over herself, last-minute poo). In 99 per cent of cases, we are late because I didn't get my act together.

I also tell untruths to my children reasonably regularly. These are what I like to think of as 'therapeutic lies', designed to ease my children's passage through life (or, you know, ease *my* passage through life). These therapeutic lies include anything that assists me to move more comfortably through my day, sidetracking disputes, bypassing convoluted explanations, and avoiding awkward discussions about topics that none of us are yet ready to broach.

## Therapeutic Lies

- That noise you can hear through the walls is just the neighbour exercising. She really likes exercising.
- Babies are made from love.
- That drink I have every afternoon at five o'clock is my special health juice. It is very important that I drink it all up.

🐞 *This isn't chocolate. It is brown tofu. You won't like it at all.*

🐞 *No, Daddy and I aren't arguing. We are just rehearsing for a play we are in.*

🐞 *I didn't sleep on the couch this morning. I just got up really early to watch a movie. On, er, DVD.*

🐞 *If you don't go to school, I will have to go to jail.*

🐞 *If you don't sit still in the car, we will all have to go to jail.*

🐞 *If you don't brush your teeth, they will turn green and fall out.*

🐞 *Oops! Daddy fell on top of me on the bed when we were trying to put on our pyjamas.*

🐞 *That funny smell is just incense. Don't get too close.*

🐞 *No, I'm not crying. I've just got something caught in my eye.*

🐞 *No, of course I don't hate your friend. I just got a fright when I saw how pretty she is.*

🐞 *No, I don't hate your friend's mummy! When I said 'bitch' I was talking about her lovely doggy.*

🐞 *Of course I love all of Daddy's relatives, especially your Grandma Mary. I just prefer to stay away from her so that she can concentrate on playing with you.*

🐞 *No, I wasn't swearing. I was practising speaking Swedish.*

🐞 *Go back to sleep! I'm fine, I'm just falling over and laughing hysterically because Daddy said something really, really funny.*

🐞 *No, these aren't legs from a real chicken. They are different legs. They grow in the ground. Like trees.*

🐞 *Yes, I was listening to every single word you said.*

🐞 *No, I didn't fall asleep in your concert! You must have just looked over at me when I was blinking.*

🐞 *Oh yes, I love playing Monopoly. The longer the game the better.*

🐞 *Oh, I love your choice of outfit. The green wellingtons look especially good with the pink tutu and the blue and orange cardigan.*

🐞 *School is fantastic! You'll love it!*

🐞 *This medicine doesn't taste bad at all.*

# Not My Children

*C*hildren can be a parent's greatest pride and joy. I, for one, am desperately proud of my own children.

There have been many times in my life when my children have made me literally weep with pride. Watching Pinkela sing in the junior choir (even when she forgot to sing and started waving to us in the audience). Watching Little Man win every maths prize his school could bestow. Watching the two older children in the school play (especially when Toddler ran up to the stage gleefully calling their names). Watching the big kids look after their baby sister. Just seeing them be the divine people that they are.

So besotted am I that I have become one of those tragic mothers who take out photographs of their children and show them to friends, family, work colleagues, taxi drivers, supermarket cashiers, doctors, hairdressers – pretty much anyone who provides a captive audience. I know that these people have about as little interest in the appearance of my offspring as I do in theirs, which is less than zero. And yet I am compelled to do so, probably because in photographs, my kids look darn near perfect.

My children are gorgeous, hilarious, and clever. They can also be cheeky, embarrassing, and downright rude. Most significantly, they can be ruthlessly honest, which is an endearing quality, except when the honesty reflects badly on me.

Despite the countless moments of delight, there have been countless other occasions over the years when my magnificent children have made me wish to run and hide.

## Top Sixteen Moments of Mortification

(I aimed for a Top Ten, but there were simply too many...)

1  *Little Man merrily announced to his preschool teacher, 'Daddy yell and Mummy cry!' (May I state for the record that this was quite unfair, as it had been our first argument in a year. Okay, a month. Okay, a week...)*

2  *Pinkela sobbed hysterically when meeting a new babysitter, saying, 'I don't like the way she looks!'*

3  *Little Man informed my grandfather matter-of-factly that, 'Eighty is a good time to die!' (My grandfather was, at the time, eighty-six.)*

4  *Pinkela told a cashier at the supermarket, 'Mummy did a poo-poo on the potty this morning.' The cashier warmly congratulated me.*

5  *Pinkela announced to her grandmother, 'When you take the "o" out of "count" you get a rude word!'*

6  *Little Man declared in front of a friend, 'Mum, you promised we wouldn't stay with her long. We just have to do our duty and leave!'*

7  *Little Man told his friend Robbie, 'Mum doesn't like me going to your house because she thinks your mum is a nightmare.' (In my defence, Robbie's mum is a nightmare.)*

8  *Pinkela told a little Asian girl, 'You have to meet my friend Kim – you look exactly like her!'*

9   Little Man confided in an insecure babysitter, 'Mum got you today because the one we really like couldn't come.'

10  Pinkela greeted an elderly, rather cumbersome woman politely with the cheerful salutation, 'Hello, fat old lady!'

11  Toddler screamed all the way through a five-hour flight after I confidently told the nearby passengers, 'Don't worry – she'll sleep the whole time.'

12  Upon seeing an elderly relative after an absence of some months, Little Man whispered audibly, 'Oh, I thought he was dead!'

13  Pinkela lifted up my shirt in public and announced to the world, 'Mum has a baby in her tummy!' ... when I didn't.

14  Pinkela ran up to a little boy and lifted her shirt and announced, 'I have sexy boobies!' ... when she didn't.

15  Little Man picked a toy off a supermarket shelf and asked loudly, 'Mum, can't we just steal it?'

16  Toddler stood with me in a toilet stall in a crowded public bathroom yelling, 'Do a poo, Mummy! DO A POO RIGHT NOW!'

# Crime and Punishment

*B*efore I had children I knew I'd be a marvellous disciplinarian. I was highly experienced with child-rearing, having babysat numerous kids after they had gone to sleep. (And yes, I can see now that this possibly didn't give me as much expertise as I believed at the time.) More importantly, I had spent time with other people's children in the presence of their parents, and could see very clearly what those other people were doing wrong. All their kids' bad behaviours were clearly due to their failings as parents. They were too strict, or too lenient. Too rigid, or too inconsistent. Too by the book, or too haphazard. I certainly wasn't going to make *their* mistakes.

No, I would be different. I would never threaten my children, or scream at them, or smack them, or lash out in anger. I would be controlled and thoughtful. I would use rewards and incentives, never bribes (although, to be honest, I wasn't 100 per cent sure I knew the difference). I would use punishments appropriate to the age of the child. I would use time-out (because I'd heard it was a very effective tool). And I would use love (although, to be honest, I didn't really know what using 'love' as a means of discipline actually meant).

Basically, I was going to get it right.

And you know what? I did. Over the past eleven years, I

have completely mastered my disciplinary techniques. Just, for some strange reason, they generally do not work.

## Beyond Discipline

*Star Charts:*
Ah, yes … these are so incredibly effective initially. Little Man clamours for stars. He offers to do chores. He clamours for more stars. Then he clamours again. And again. And again. Again and again. Around seventeen times an hour until the very word 'star' makes me want to stab myself with a fork. And God forbid he thinks he's done something wrong, because then panic ensues: 'Am I getting a star taken away, Mum? Can I get it back? *How* can I get it back? *When* can I get it back?' So incessantly does my son talk about the bloody stars that I have to threaten to take them away if he asks for them again. Which he inevitably does. So I inevitably do. Which results in a total meltdown that pretty much defeats the whole purpose of the exercise.

Pinkela, on the other hand, couldn't care less about stars, and is just as well or as badly behaved whether she receives them or not And Toddler? She just pulls them off the chart and eats them.

*Rewards/Incentives:*
Incentives work brilliantly for my children, as long as they are happy to do whatever it is I'm rewarding them to do (using 'rewarding' in the sense of 'bribing', as I still haven't figured out the difference). They'll perform their task cheerfully and return to normal business with a prize they hadn't asked for and didn't need. However, if my kids don't want to do something, then all the incentives in the world won't make them

do it. I could offer them each a Wii and a jumping castle filled with chocolate, but if they are disinclined to have their shower or clean their room or visit Aunt Mabel, then I might as well be offering them a carrot (a real carrot, not a metaphorical one). They will listen, screw up their noses, and politely decline.

As for Toddler, the reward system is completely ineffective. Offer her a chocolate incentive and she will weep, wail and vomit until she gets it, without showing even the slightest intention of doing what you want her to do.

*Teaching Right from Wrong:*
I'm very proud to say that my three children all know their right from wrong. Unfortunately, however, this doesn't actually make them choose to do right instead of wrong. Sometimes the wrong thing is far more fun to do. Sometimes it just feels really good to be bad, even if you know it will make your mummy sad and cross.

I wasn't at all prepared for this pre-parenthood. I assumed that if you taught kids right from wrong, then your job as a parent was complete.

On the positive side, at least I get pre-emptive apologies. 'Sorry for doing this, Mummy,' says Toddler, as she empties a full bottle of bath gel into the tub.

'Mummy, you're going to be very cross at me for this,' says Pinkela, before telling me about her latest misadventures in class.

'Yes, I hit her. I'm going to my room now,' says Little Man, before stomping off to his bedroom.

Okay, so maybe they haven't altered their behaviour, but at least I don't have to tell them how bad they've been, right? *Right?*

*Speaking Sternly:*
For some reason (probably because pretty much everything else I try fails), Speaking Sternly has become my default disciplinary tool. 'Put that down RIGHT NOW!' I will command, marvelling to myself at how freakishly like a mother I actually sound. The fact that it never works hasn't in the least deterred me, which I think says a great deal about my persistence in the face of resistance.

It doesn't matter how loudly I speak, or how softly but menacingly I whisper; my children just do not respond. Clearly, they are suffering from some kind of selective hearing impediment, no doubt inherited from their father, The Architect. Little Man, for example, will hear the word 'Nintendo' from fifty metres away, but cannot hear the words 'TV off' spoken right next to his ear. And Pinkela, who can memorise TV shows after one viewing, cannot seem to absorb any instructions that come from a live human being in front of her face. 'Get. Dressed. NOW!' I'll tell her, from a distance of ten centimetres, approximately seventeen times in a row. Eventually she'll get up and amble off in the direction of her bedroom, only to be found five minutes later meandering around the house with a sock in one hand asking, 'What I am meant to be doing?' If I Speak Sternly to her at this point in the process, she will look up at me with her huge eyes and a deeply wounded expression on her face and say, 'You don't have to yell at me, Mummy!'

As for Toddler, well, Speaking Sternly doesn't work at all. She'll either weep, which just makes me weep, or grin, sing 'Mee Po!' (no, you haven't heard of it; it's a song she made up), throw her blanky over her head and then ask merrily for juice. Or dance, depending on her mood.

*Smacking:*

Smacking works brilliantly for my kids. Sadly, however, it doesn't work in the sense of 'marvellously effective disciplinary technique', but rather in the sense of 'Woo hoo, I've got the better of Mum!' You see, on the rare occasions that I have actually smacked one of my children, I have always felt racked with guilt and ended up self-flagellating and apologising, which is probably not the most helpful response when your child has deliberately drawn on the walls in black marker pen, or stomped on his sister's foot under the table.

Better just stick to the star charts.

# Time for Bed

There are many things you can force a recalcitrant child to do. You can force them to get dressed. You can force them to go to school. You can force them to clean their room. You can even force them to eat, if you are so inclined (although, as you cannot prevent them from throwing up afterwards, this doesn't come without risks). However, as any parent will learn very quickly, there are a couple of things you can't force a child to do.

You cannot make your child poo if they don't want to poo. And you can never, ever, force a child to sleep.

There is a certain desperation associated with a child's sleep time, generally because it corresponds with the period at which parents have reached their limits and are longing for a break. The longer the child remains awake, the shorter that break will be. And yet, it is notoriously difficult to get a child to go to sleep. So much so, that a 'good sleeper' has become the most coveted prize among parents, the baby that all mothers desire. Smart kids, attractive kids, talented kids, sporty kids ... they're all very nice, but what we really want are offspring who will leave us alone for twelve hours out of every day. Willingly.

Of course, for most of us, this is but a pipedream. Trying to get the kids to bed at night is like teaching them to ride a bike:

there are a lot of false starts and failures before their triumphant cycle off into the sunset of sleep. However, unlike bike riding, we have to teach them to sleep, night after night, for about ten to fifteen years.

## Getting My Kids to Sleep: A Timeline

**8.00:** *The children are immersed in TV. It is late. I am tired. 'Five more minutes, guys, then bedtime!' I announce brightly. There is no response. Five minutes pass.*

**8.05:** *'Okay, time for bed!' I announce again. There is no response. 'TIME. FOR. BED!' I yell. The kids look up languidly. 'No need to yell,' says Pinkela, looking hurt.*

**8.10:** *'Okay, BEDTIME!' I announce again, firmly. I switch off the TV. 'DON'T TURN THE TV OFF!' Little Man screams. 'THAT'S MY FAVOURITE PART!' 'You can record it,' I tell him. 'NOOOOO,' he yells, getting increasingly agitated. I realise that he'll never sleep in this condition. 'Okay, five more minutes,' I inform him. 'Yay!' he says brightly. Twenty minutes pass.*

**8.30:** *'BEDTIME!' I announce. 'In one sec,' says Little Man. Ten minutes pass.*

**8.40:** *'BEDTIME NOW!' I yell. 'FINE,' Little Man says, and stomps off sullenly to his room. 'You don't have to yell,' says Pinkela, looking hurt. 'Milky! Milky!' yells Toddler. Oh, Toddler. I had forgotten about her. 'You've already had milky,' I tell her. 'I want MORE!' she cries. I realise she'll never sleep in this condition. 'Okay, just a bit more milky,' I inform her. 'Yay!' she says.*

**8.45:** *I give Toddler milk and go to check on Little Man. He is sitting on the floor of his bedroom sorting through his*

Pokemon cards. '*GET INTO BED!*' I shout. '*Just one sec,*' he says. I sigh and go to check on Pinkela.

**8.50:** Pinkela is sitting on her bed brushing her dolly's hair. '*GET INTO BED!*' I shout. '*Just one sec,*' she says. I sigh and go back to Toddler.

**8.52:** Toddler has spilt wet milk all over her pyjamas. I sigh and change her. '*Bedtime,*' I tell her. '*NOOOOO!*' she howls. I lift her firmly into her cot. '*Mu-MEEEEE!*' I hear her wail plaintively as I resolutely close the door.

**9.00:** Pinkela comes out of her room. '*Make her stop crying!*' she cries. I sigh. '*Brush your teeth,*' I tell her. '*But I want my milk!*' she says. '*Go get it,*' I say, '*but HURRY.*'

**9.05:** I go in to Toddler. '*Go to sleep,*' I say gently, and pat her bottom. '*Mummy loves you.*' Her tears diminish to a sniffle. I creep out the room. '*Mu-MEEEEE!*' I hear her scream. I sigh.

**9.10:** I go in to Pinkela. She has a glass of milk in her hands. '*Good night, darling,*' I say. '*But I haven't brushed my teeth,*' she tells me. '*I don't care,*' I reply.

**9.15:** I go in to Little Man. He is in bed. '*Good night, darling,*' I say. '*I forgot to do my homework,*' he tells me. '*I don't care,*' I reply.

**9.20:** I go in to Toddler. She is asleep. Realise I have forgotten to put a nappy on her. I weigh up the risks of waking her versus the risks of leaving her without a nappy. I decide I just don't care. I tiptoe up the stairs.

**9.25:** '*MUM!*' I hear.

## Not Down Yet

*O*ne of the great, tragic ironies of parenthood is that, while we mothers spend much of our lives fantasising about getting into bed, our kids spend much of their lives trying to get out of it. If only we could get our children to crave sleep as much as we do, then 90 per cent of our problems would be wiped out in one fell swoop.

Getting my kids into bed each night is only half the challenge. The rest of the challenge is to get them off to sleep. Only when they are all actually unconscious is my evening's work done (if, of course, you don't consider cleaning the kitchen, making school lunches for the next day and folding three basketfuls of laundry 'work'). And unhappily for me, this can take hours. While some nights my kids fall asleep the moment their heads hit the pillows, they frequently party in relentless agitation until the wee small hours, because – even though I am delirious with exhaustion – they simply 'can't sleep'.

But *why* can't they sleep? What difficulties befall an eleven-year-old boy to stop him from drifting off into slumber? What issues keep a nine-year-old girl awake till ten o'clock at night?

Oh, many, many reasons. And tragically, there are no effective solutions.

## *I can't sleep, Mum*

- I'm too cold.
- I'm too hot.
- It's too light.
- It's too dark.
- I'm worried about school tomorrow.
- I'm worried about the test next week.
- I'm worried about the camp next term.
- I'm worried about how the episode of The Simpsons will finish.
- I'm worried about how my Nintendo game will finish.
- I'm worried. Just worried.
- There are monsters in my cupboard.
- I'm scared I'll have a bad dream.
- I have lots of thoughts.
- I don't know what to think about.
- I feel funny.
- I need to wee.
- I need to poo.
- My leg is asleep.
- I need a hot water bottle.
- I need bedsocks.
- I'm not tired enough to sleep.
- I'm too tired to sleep.
- I'm thirsty.
- I'm hungry.
- My tummy aches because I ate too much.
- My bed is uncomfortable.
- My pillows are uncomfortable.
- My pyjamas are uncomfortable.
- I'm not comfortable. No reason. I'm just not.

# Mother's Day... Or Not

Mother's Day is purely commercial. We all know this. Mother's Day is a social construction, born of advertising geniuses who decided that it would be another clever way for retailers to make a bit of money. It's silly. It's meaningless.

And yet I still fall for it.

Why? Because I *deserve* a Mother's Day. I *need* a Mother's Day. I work hard every day to raise children who are happy, healthy, and free of (immediately discernible) emotional disturbances, and I should be recognised for my efforts.

Still, the Mother's Day that I want isn't necessarily the Mother's Day that I get. The Mother's Day that I want is the Mother's Day that I was sold: the Mother's Day of advertisements. A dewy-eyed mother embraces her rosy-cheeked children as her handsome, clean-cut husband looks on with pride. The breakfast tray is stunning, the presents are numerous and stylish, and everyone smells sweetly fragrant. (I know it's television, so I can't actually smell them, but I can just tell.)

Unfortunately, of course, this is all just fantasy. The Mother's Day of advertisements is very different to the Mother's Day of my real life, because the Mother's Day of advertisements involves stylists, make-up artists and models. The Mother's Day of my real life, on the other hand involves my real children and their real father. And they're nowhere near as perfect as the imitation.

| My Fantasy Mother's Day | My Real Mother's Day |
|---|---|
| *I wake up in a silky negligee between crisp, white sheets, with shiny hair and moisturised, glowing skin.* | *I wake up in a stained, oversized T-shirt, on sheets that haven't been washed in a fortnight, hair matted with remnants of last night's spaghetti, and my face crusted with two-day-old mascara.* |
| *I am woken by fresh-smelling, adoring children standing beside my bed, bearing gifts and wishes of love, motivated by nothing but the promise of my maternal delight.* | *I am woken by three scruffy, Vegemite-smeared children bouncing perilously close to my head, wanting me to open my presents so that I can see how clever they are, but only after I've fetched them drinks, wiped their mouths, and changed Toddler's nappy.* |
| *I receive exquisitely selected gifts of clothes, jewellery, sleepwear, chocolates, jewellery, spa vouchers, shoes, jewellery, handbags, cosmetics and jewellery, bought from a range of large chain stores and quirky little boutiques after an intensive search by my family.* | *I receive gifts from the school Mother's Day stall: a fair trade candle that melts in approximately forty-five seconds; a bag of potpourri that smells like ... well ... nothing, really; a hemp scarf with the texture of a cardboard box; and a change purse that would be lucky to fit a pound coin, let alone those inconveniently large 50p pieces. And I will cherish every single one of them. (Because my kids gave them to me. Not because they're actually any good.)* |

| My Fantasy Mother's Day | My Real Mother's Day |
| --- | --- |
| *I am served a breakfast of freshly squeezed orange juice, a skim cappuccino, perfectly poached eggs on sourdough toast with a side of spinach, presented on an elegant wooden tray with silver cutlery, a red rose in a vase, and a linen serviette.* | *I am served a breakfast of supermarket orange juice, cold white toast with Vegemite, and a tepid cup of instant coffee with about seventeen spoons of sugar, on a plastic tray sprinkled with crumbs. And I eat the lot. (Except for the coffee, which I discreetly tip down the bathroom sink when no one is watching.)* |
| *I spend the day at a spa, where I am massaged, cleansed, buffed, painted, renewed, refreshed and rejuvenated, before returning home to my delightful, happy children who have prepared a nutritious but delicious evening meal under the tutelage of their father, prior to putting themselves to bed and leaving me to watch re-runs of* The Mentalist *in blissed-out peace before retiring for an early night.* | *I get to spend the whole day with my own kids, performing all the functions that I would normally perform as a mother, with the exception that I do so with the constant refrain of, 'Did you like the breakfast? Did you like my present?' ringing in my ears. And I love it. Every minute of it. Although I would really have liked that day spa experience, too.* |

# Twelve Years of Lunch Boxes

## A Curriculum of TV

*I* admire people who homeschool their children (using 'admire' in the sense of 'think they're not quite right in the head'). And I'm sure that homeschooling has many advantages. After all, you won't go through a dozen lunch boxes a term, you won't experience the shame of getting your kids to school late, and you won't need to buy ridiculously expensive blazers, which will be pulled out of the bottom of the cupboard and worn approximately once, before being lost during the first excursion.

I would, however, make a terrible homeschooler. Not only am I completely unqualified for the task, but the very idea fills me with horror. If the school system ever collapsed and homeschooling was the only remaining option, my children would need to resign themselves to a curriculum of television and Nintendo, in preparation for careers in envelope stuffing. The chances of me becoming a competent teacher are less than zero. In fact, I'd be far more likely to grow a second head.

## Why I'll Never Homeschool

🐸 If my children have only one teacher in their lives, it shouldn't be one whose primary areas of speciality are nappy changing, speed shopping, and sweeping under the carpet (both literally and metaphorically).

🐸 If my children have only one teacher in their lives, it shouldn't be one whose library consists of books with names like Taming the Angry Child, 75 Ways with Mince, and How to Save the Unsalvageable Marriage.

🐸 The only topic I am motivated to teach my children is 'How to Clean the House and Do Laundry'. At this stage this not an assessable component of the primary school curriculum. Nor is 'Nap Time', 'Nappy Time' or 'Snack Time' – the only other areas in which I feel confident.

🐸 My general knowledge is woeful. The only languages I speak fluently are English and Toddler, with a smattering of Teletubby. My knowledge of music is limited to The Wiggles, Love Song Dedications, Eminem (I know, I'm nothing if not esoteric) and 'Happy Birthday to You' (which Toddler inexplicably sings to everyone she meets). And my knowledge of history is limited to ... well ... around five minutes ago. After three kids, I can barely remember what I did this morning, let alone what happened last week, ten years ago, or in the First World War.

🐸 I get exhausted just getting my kids ready for school. If I had to be the school, I would be asleep by noon.

🐸 It's bad enough making school lunches for the kids. Having to watch them eat their school lunches would send me right over the edge.

🐸 The only science experiment I have ever conducted began as an attempt to cook a cheese soufflé. In other words, I am a failure at science and home economics.

🐞 *The only excursions I am prepared to conduct are not especially educational (unless you consider He's Just Not That into You and Sex and the City educational films).*

🐞 *I feel unqualified to teach physical education as I have not engaged in formal exercise since 1993.*

🐞 *I feel unqualified to teach geography as I get lost driving to the swimming carnival each year.*

🐞 *I feel unqualified to teach life skills as I still have tantrums when things go wrong.*

🐞 *If my kids are with me all day long, they will witness my frequent nervous breakdowns, and will require even more expensive therapy than they already do. What's more, if I am the one educating them, then there is very little likelihood that as adults they will be able to afford any therapy at all.*

🐞 *I simply cannot be around my children all day long.*

# Parents Go to School Too

*I* was terribly excited when my children started school. I thought this would be a new beginning for me – a chance to throw myself back into work, reconnect with the adult world, maybe even spend some time alone. (I know! Can you imagine? Alone!) I envisioned long, lazy days, dropping the kids at school, returning home to tidy the house, before doing a few hours' work, meeting a friend for lunch, and squeezing in a manicure in the afternoon.

Oh, how I laugh at those foolish plans. Oh, how I mock my younger, naive self, who saw school as a chance to reclaim herself. Once again, I was so very, very wrong.

As it turns out, by the time I drop my kids off at their schools, I have approximately fifteen minutes to get things done before I have to return to pick them up again. Okay, so I'm exaggerating slightly. I actually have around six and a half hours, but considering the amount of chores I need to get through in that time, it may as well be fifteen minutes. In the average six-and-a-half-hour day, I need to clean the kitchen, do three loads of laundry, change sheets on at least one bed, pick up some groceries, pay some bills, run to the bank/chemist/drycleaner/doctor's, do some work, prepare dinner, return emails, and find time to do a wee. And if I have a lengthy meeting or an appointment that runs overtime, the likelihood is that tonight we're going to be eating toast.

Unfortunately, it's not just the school day that is ridiculously short. School terms last for only five weeks (or so it seems), and out of the entire school year there are only about twenty or thirty school days in which parental presence is not required. It seems that virtually every week, parents must go to school for one reason or another. Mother's Day, Parents' Day, Show and Tell Day, Open Day, Concert Evening ... it's relentless.

Of course, there is no pressure to attend. No pressure at all. But try *not* attending and see what happens. You'll find yourself comforting a weeping seven-year-old who claims that she was the 'only one who didn't have a mummy at the swimming carnival!' or a son who is 'very disappointed you didn't watch all five rounds of my chess tournament' or a Toddler who looks tragically alone in pictures of Dress-Up Day at crèche. (Who the hell knew parents are meant to attend Dress-Up Day anyway?)

You'll also need to deal with vigilantes from the PTA, who corner you at school pick-up time to 'request' your assistance to serve hot dogs at the Sausage Sizzle Charity Morning, or to wrap presents at the Father's Day stall, or to decorate the hall for the End-of-Year Disco, or to do any number of extracurricular chores for which Good Mothers cheerfully volunteer their services without any prompting at all.

Clearly, I am not a Good Mother.

## Attendance is Compulsory

🧸 *For tuckshop duty, to make sandwiches, dole out change, fetch iceblocks, and tend to the gastronomic requirements of several hundred children instead of the three I normally deal with.*

🐻 At Meet the Teacher nights, where I learn all about the marvellous curricula my kids will be studying this term (which I will learn all about anyway as I do the homework with them. Or for them).

🐻 At parent–teacher interviews, twice a year, for each child, and an extra two or three times a term during those, ahem, 'challenging' periods.

🐻 At excursions as the parent helper, for which I hold the dubious distinction of being the only person ever to actually lose a child on a school outing (despite the fact that I had only three children in my care).

🐻 At special assemblies, where I get to watch my child participate for four minutes, then watch other people's children receive awards for the next thirty.

🐻 At sports and swimming carnivals, in order to cheer Little Man's house on to victory, even if he has the sporting prowess of an earthworm and comes last in the one race in which he competes.

🐻 At school plays, even if Pinkela appears for approximately two minutes only, in the second-last scene of a three-hour performance, wearing a bright red tomato suit, lost in a sea of twenty other bright red tomatoes.

🐻 At school concerts, where I experience the cringing delight of hearing Pinkela play the violin very badly; and the torment of hearing other people's children play even worse.

🐻 To help set up on 'special occasions' such as Concert Evenings, Father's Day, End-of-Year Barbecues, and the 20,000 other 'special occasions' that occur each year.

# Assemble Here

'Special Assemblies' take a particular toll on the parents in attendance, or at least they sure as hell took their toll on me.

I had to attend 'special assemblies' until both Little Man and Pinkela reached Year Three, and will do so again once Toddler starts school. Once a term, each class in the infants department is required to present a special 'item' at assembly. Naturally, all the parents of that class are invited (read, 'ordered') to watch and marvel. So, once a term, the parents are taken on a great roller-coaster of emotion. There are moments of intense pleasure interspersed with moments of great anxiety. Tensions run high.

Consider one of Pinkela's earliest efforts. The theme of her class's performance (using the term 'performance' with its original Latin meaning of 'confused and disordered congregation on stage') was 'Things I Am Good At'.

One by one the five-year-olds held up pictures of their special skills and shared their talents rather loudly with the audience. 'I'm good at jumping!' yelled one child. 'I'm good at throwing porridge!' screamed another. (Or at least I think that's what she said; I was covering my ears at the time.)

My heart was pounding with nerves as Pinkela approached the microphone. What if she forgot her lines, or fell over, or walked off the stage in disgust as her brother had done two years earlier? Or – God forbid – what if she wasn't actually good at anything?

'I'm good at reading, writing AND making friends!' my little girl bellowed. Praise the Lord! My heart nearly burst with pride. Of course, Pinkela couldn't actually read at the time, and the only word she could write was her name, but these minor details I kept discreetly to myself.

Following Pinkela's performance was the presentation of Praise Certificates. I longed, with arguably inappropriate desperation, to see my son receive an award. Obviously he had received many of them over the years (again using the term 'many' with its original Latin meaning of 'very, very few') but never in my presence, and, as he was soon moving up to the junior school, time was running out.

Every time a name was called out my heart would leap with anticipation, then plummet in despair. Still, I tried to be happy for the recipients. *To Jake, in Year One, for Always Doing His Best.* Well done, Jake. *To Millie, in Year Two, for Doing Good Work in English.* Yay, Millie...

But as the list continued and my son wasn't mentioned, I became more than a little resentful. *To Katy, in Year One, for Being a Happy Class Member.* Happy? Well, excuse me, but as far as I know 'happy' just doesn't cut it in the real world. 'Katy, we're giving you a pay rise because you're such a *happy* employee. Your work is crap but you're just so cheerful!'

*To Ben, in Year Two, for Always Raising His Hand to Ask a Question.* Fabulous, Ben. You're really going to do well in life with that skill. 'Congratulations, Ben, we're promoting you, because you always raise your hand when you ask a question!'

Then Louis got an award for doing well in French and I really lost the plot. Louis? His parents are *from* France! Of course he'd do well in French! This was getting outrageous. What kind of school were my kids attending?

And then the last Praise Certificate was presented. All hope was lost. I slumped down in my chair.

'And finally, a certificate for a Year Two student, for Excellence in Problem Solving... A–'

It was him! My son! I leaped out of my seat, punching the air, in a manner reminiscent of Tom Cruise on *The Oprah Show*. My heart ached with joy as Little Man beamed at me with pride and the mother next to me retreated slightly in fear.

My kids' school assemblies were a wonderful experience, and I am eternally grateful that I don't have to attend one for another several years. As much as I love seeing my children perform, if I have to live through that trauma again every term for the next three years, I definitely won't make it through to high school.

# Homework Hell

*O*f course, even those of us who don't homeschool are still required to school at home. No matter how vehemently we resist the pull, no matter how hopelessly ill-equipped we are to do the job, we parents of school-aged children will inevitably be sucked into the vortex that is homework.

Now, not all children need help to do their homework. There are kids who will take themselves off to their rooms at four p.m., happily complete their maths and comprehension quizzes, and then reappear an hour later relaxed and ready to curl up on the couch with an improving book.

But these children, as we all know, are bizarro freaks.

The majority of children (i.e. mine) require a parent to sit down with them at the table (using 'sit down with' in the sense of 'tether') and supervise every second of the homework experience. The minutes tick by agonisingly slowly as Little Man grizzles, moans, tears his hair, and shouts about how unfair the world is, Pinkela bites her pen, stares dreamily into space, and asks, 'What am I supposed to be doing again?', and Toddler yells for TV and scribbles furiously on her siblings' completed work.

And homework time isn't just painful and tedious. By the time my son got to Year Four it also became exceedingly demoralising, as this was the time the school curriculum overtook my general knowledge. Though happily I am still able to help with spelling and basic arithmetic, all other subjects, particularly science, history, geometry, foreign languages and something called 'personal development' are utterly beyond me. In fact, if it wasn't for the miraculous invention of Google, I may have had to hire a tutor for myself.

## What My Kids Say About Homework

- I hate homework.
- This is boring.
- This is stupid.
- This is too easy.
- This is too hard.
- This isn't fair.
- Why do I have to do homework?
- I've been at school all day and now I have to work more.
- Can you just read it out to me?
- Can you just write it down for me?
- Can you just look it up for me?
- Can you just tell me if it's right?
- Can you just tell me the answer?
- Can I get up now?
- I'll do one more and that's it.

## What I Say about Homework

- I'm NOT doing any more.
- You have to do it.
- Just do it.
- Do it and I'll give you a treat.

🐾 *Do it and you can play Game Boy.*

🐾 *Do it or you won't get any TV tonight.*

🐾 *Do it or you'll get into trouble at school.*

🐾 *If you don't do your homework, you'll fail all your subjects and you'll never amount to anything.*

🐾 *Fine, don't do it. See if I care.*

🐾 *I hate homework, too.*

🐾 *I did my homework. Now it's your turn.*

🐾 *Okay, I'll read it out to you.*

🐾 *Okay, I'll write it down for you.*

🐾 *No, I WON'T give you the answers.*

🐾 *Okay, I'll just give you the first answer and you can work out the rest.*

🐾 *Are you sure that's right?*

# The Children Have Lapsed into Comas

The most challenging aspect of school is not the homework, or the assemblies. The most challenging aspect of school is trying to get the kids there on time. So challenging, in fact, that it virtually never happens in my family. It is disgraceful but true: my children are almost always late for school.

Now, I know that I am the mother and it is my responsibility to ensure my kids arrive at school before breaktime. And I'll be honest: I am rather disorganised and have a worrying propensity to sleep through my alarm. However, there are other factors working against me. Such as my children's extreme reluctance to get off the couch. The Architect's inability to assist with getting them ready. (He is, apparently, 'not good' in the mornings.) The tendency of my keys to get lost as we are leaving the house. Toddler's fondness for doing a poo just as we get into the car. And then, of course, the school's ridiculously early starting time of eight-twenty. I mean, really. I've got three children! How can I possibly be expected to get anywhere by eight-twenty?

## Getting The Kids to School: A Timeline

**6.30:** My alarm wakes me with a piercing screech. I must leave the house at eight a.m. to get to school by eight-twenty. I have ninety minutes. Plenty of time.

**6.31:** I turn the alarm off and immediately fall back into a deep sleep.

**7.16:** I wake up with Toddler bouncing on my head screaming, 'Mum, Mum, WAKE UP! Mum, you sleepy?'

**7.18:** I stumble out of bed and trip on Pinkela's Barbie.

**7.19:** I walk down the corridor and trip on Little Man's High-Bounce Ball.

**7.20:** I enter the lounge room to find the older kids slumped on the couch in their pyjamas watching an X-rated episode of The Simpsons.

**7.22:** I yell at the children to hurry up and get dressed. There is no response. I momentarily panic, convinced the children have lapsed into comas.

**7.23:** I block the television so that the kids are forced to see me. I stand there and refuse to give way until they agree to tell me what they will eat for breakfast. Eventually, they request pancakes.

**7.26:** I tell them there is no time for pancakes and ask them to choose something else. Eventually, they request cheese on toast.

**7.28:** I go into the kitchen and realise that a) I am out of bread, and b) I am out of cheese. I make the kids cornflakes.

**7.31:** When they complain I add some Nesquik, and tell them that it's flat Coco Pops.

**7.32:** I rush to find their uniforms. Unsurprisingly (as it happens twice a week), Pinkela's school shoes are missing. I go on a frenzied search of the house, before finding one of the shoes in the shower and the other in her rubbish bin.

**7.35:** *I fling the uniforms in the general direction of the children, calling, 'Get dressed while I'm in the shower!' over my shoulder as I run to the bathroom.*

**7.36:** *I enter the bathroom to find The Architect in the shower. I sigh.*

**7.37:** *I throw on some dirty clothes from the previous day and spray my body liberally with deodorant to mask the smell.*

**7.41:** *I run back to the children who are sitting slack-jawed in their pyjamas surrounded by pools of milk and cornflakes.*

**7.42:** *I throw a tea towel over the pools of milk and cornflakes. I decide I'll get to it later.*

**7.43:** *I scream some more. 'You don't have to yell' says Little Man, accusingly.*

**7.44:** *I dress all three kids myself, despite the fact that the eldest is eleven.*

**7.50:** *I feel a dull headache descend and my sight begins to go blurry. I make myself a coffee and drink it standing up in the kitchen. Almost instantaneously, I am cured.*

**7.53:** *I realise that Little Man is wearing the wrong socks. I decide it is best not to mention it. I yell at the kids to pack their bags. 'You don't have to yell,' says Pinkela, reproachfully.*

**7.54:** *I give up and pack the kids' bags myself, then yell at them to brush their teeth. 'Why you yell, Mama?' asks Toddler.*

**7.59:** *The children return with (reasonably) clean teeth. 'Okay, let's go!' I say.*

**8.00:** *'But, Mum, you haven't made us any lunch!' cries Pinkela. 'But, Mum, you haven't signed my homework book!' cries Little Man. 'But, Mum, I haven't done my homework!' cries Pinkela. 'But, Mama, I haven't done homework, too!' cries Toddler. I fight the urge to run screaming from the family home.*

**8.01:** *The Architect strolls into the kitchen drying his hair with a towel. 'Can you iron me a shirt?' he asks nonchalantly. I look longingly at my keys.*

**8.02:** *'Mum, we're LATE!' the kids chorus. 'HURRY!'*

**8.03:** *I make lunches out of crackers and Vegemite. 'Yum, you're having crispy sandwiches today,' I say brightly.*

**8.08:** *I sign Little Man's homework book while quickly doing Pinkela's maths homework.*

**8.10:** *I tell The Architect that there's a clean shirt waiting for him at the laundromat, an easy thirty-five-minute drive from work.*

**8.11:** *I hustle the kids out to the car, after scraping last night's pumpkin soup stains from their uniforms.*

**8.12:** *Once in the car, Toddler announces, 'I done a big poo-poo! Change my undies! Change my undies!' The smell is overpowering.*

**8.13:** *I run back inside with Toddler, studiously avoiding The Architect who is still roaming around shirtless and confused. I clean her up, change her undies and return to the car.*

**8.18:** *Little Man announces that he has left his clarinet inside.*

**8.19:** *I run back inside to fetch the clarinet. The Architect is wearing an old grey T-shirt with his suit. He does not look happy.*

**8.20:** *I return to the car. Pinkela announces that she has left her library book inside. I tell her to get an extension.*

**8.21:** *I drive to school avoiding the twenty-mile-per-hour school zones as, quite frankly, that is a ridiculous speed limit, and I can't possibly be expected to stick to it. Besides, my licence has been taken away once already.*

**8.37:** *Once at school, Little Man announces that he has a bad headache. I get the Panadol out of the glove box, feed him a big dose, and instruct him not to tell his teacher that he's taken it.*

**8.39:** *I wave goodbye as the two kids walk inside the school gates, nineteen minutes late.*

**8.57:** *When I return home with Toddler, I find both lunch boxes sitting on the kitchen counter.*

# Summoned

*I* don't like parent–teacher interviews. They always give me the uncomfortable feeling that I am being called into the teacher's office (which, obviously, I am). And, despite the fact that I am there to discuss my offspring and not myself, I experience the same conflict that I did is a child: of longing desperately to impress while simultaneously itching to rebel. I want to show the teacher that I am a thoughtful, conscientious, intelligent mother who works hard to maximise my child's potential. At the same time, I want to sit back in my chair and challenge her on issues with which I disagree. Even on issues with which I don't disagree. Because I'm the adult now. And I *can*.

What's more, being back in the classroom evokes painful memories for me that I have repressed since my school days. I find myself panicking that I haven't studied hard enough for my exams (which, in those days, I generally hadn't). I become nervous about asking to go to the toilet. I start remembering how horrid those toilets actually were. I feel suddenly insecure about the shoes I am wearing and the length of my skirt. And I experience that same, strong, unrequited passion for Josh Goldenbum that consumed me for most of my schooling (after I'd got over my passion for Leo Whitman, that is).

And yet ... there's more.

## I Don't Want to Go to School

- Pinkela's teacher looks approximately fourteen years old. This does not make me feel particularly confident. Or particularly young.

- I am expected to show a tremendous interest in Pinkela's fifty-page Work Samples Folder, which to my untrained eye looks like page after monotonous page of handwriting, spelling, maths and the occasional drawing (which, as it turns out, is exactly what it is). Now I love my daughter deeply but all I really want to know is if she a) has any friends, b) is normal, and c) needs any remedial attention.

- I feel remarkably ill at ease in the teensy, tiny seat (which is not surprising, because it barely accommodates my bottom).

- I notice that every other child's exercise book is perfectly covered in contact paper. Pinkela's exercise book looks like it is covered in bubble wrap (which is not surprising, because it was me who covered it).

- I worry the teacher will wish to discuss the day Pinkela said, 'Mummy called Daddy the f-word.'

- I'm worried the teacher will bring up Pinkela's Holiday Journal, which refers to her eating McDonald's six times and watching endless hours of TV.

- I'm worried the teacher will mention that Pinkela is always late for school. As she is not old enough to drive, this is probably more my fault than hers.

- I'm worried the teacher will chastise me for never signing Pinkela's homework diary or listening to her read. What can I say? I get distracted a lot. I'll try harder next time, I promise!

*Fun and Games*

# Open House

*I*'m not what you would call a pushy mother. If my kids are good at something, I'm pleased; if they're not, that's fine, too. And while I'd be perfectly delighted for them to be smart, talented and athletic, there's only one thing that I care about, one thing that I believe is the keystone to happiness.

I want them to have friends.

For this reason, I love the idea of an open house. I want the kind of home that will encourage other people's children to drop around spontaneously for a play. I want to potter around in my kitchen making cupcakes and fruit platters, listening to the sounds of delighted chatter as my kids play with their friends. I want to make pizzas and lay out pillows and blankets for the little guests at an impromptu sleepover party. It sounds like the perfect way to spend an evening.

In theory, anyway.

In practice, it's a nightmare. I mean, I'm sure there are kids who are easy, who come round and play nicely – kick a ball around, make a playhouse, play with dolls, create play dough masterpieces – but for some reason my offspring don't attract too many of them. No, my children attract friends who are kind of demanding: kids who get bored, kids who need attention, kids who don't like our toys, or kids who simply have really annoying faces.

Having said that, my own children aren't all that easy, either. Little Man in particular has been known to dismiss his friends abruptly when he has tired of playing with them – often a mere half-hour after they have arrived. 'It's time for him to leave, Mum,' he'll announce matter-of-factly, leaving the poor kid sadly looking at his feet (or staring keenly at the phone). It can take a great deal of encouragement and supervision to get the play date back on track, and keep the child at our place for the requisite two hours.

Even successful play dates can be utterly exhausting. Add another child or two to my brood, mix in some excitement, spread some chaos, and stir in sustenance every twenty minutes, and you'll find me lying on the couch at the end of the day, needing a stiff drink. And if the play date goes badly, I might just need two.

## Bad Dates

🌂 *The guest arrives at my home and expresses horror that we have no Wii.*

🌂 *The guest arrives at my home and expresses horror that we have no pool.*

🌂 *The guest arrives at my home and expresses horror that we have no Barbie Go-a-Matic Luxury Deluxe Mega Holiday Trailer and Zoo.*

🌂 *The guest arrives at my home and announces, 'There is nothing to do here.'*

🌂 *After half an hour the guest announces, 'I want to go home.'*

🌂 *After half an hour Little Man announces, 'I want him to go home.'*

🥿 *The guest is gluten-intolerant/lactose-intolerant/macrobiotic/ vegan/kosher/only eats white foods.*

🥿 *The guest looks in my fridge and pantry and announces, 'There is nothing to eat here.'*

🥿 *The guest eats everything in my fridge and pantry and then asks for more.*

🥿 *After his mother assures me he won't need anything to eat, the guest spends the next two hours begging for food.*

🥿 *After his mother assures me he will be picked up by lunchtime, the guest is still in my care at nine p.m. that night.*

🥿 *The guest encourages my kids to perform acts of pure evil involving the dishwasher, some bubble mix, and our pet bunny, Spunky.*

🥿 *The guest encourages my kids to say rude words.*

🥿 *The guest encourages Toddler to say rude words.*

🥿 *The guest swears that his parents allow him to watch X-rated movies/play with knives/light matches/drink energy drinks/ drink alcohol/use the f-word.*

🥿 *I am driven to make a late-night call to the guest's parents during a sleepover, asking them to pick him up as, 'He isn't having much fun,' which, as we parents all know, is code for, 'He hit my daughter, threw the pizza on the floor and told me my house is ugly. I've had enough.'*

# Are We Having Fun Yet?

*L*ike any mother, I want my kids to be happy. It gives me enormous pleasure to take my kids on a special outing, and to see them running around enjoying themselves. Interestingly, however, this pleasure can be quite subtle, and can coexist very nicely with excruciating, mind-numbing boredom.

Taking my kids to the playground is a prime example. On the one hand, it is delightful to sit on a bench for two hours and watch my kids have such a marvellous time. On the other hand, it is mind-numbingly boring to sit on a bench for two hours and watch my kids have such a marvellous time. I mean, it's great that they're happy and all that, but really – what is in it for me?

I hate the playground. I admit it; I do. The only exception to me hating the playground is when I'm standing in it with a bunch of other mums, takeaway cappuccino in hand, muffin in mouth, talking about how much I hate the playground. I don't like to admit I hate it, because I want to be seen as a Good Mother who really cares about my children, but underneath the facade of good-mothering I totally do.

And who can blame me?

## Why I Hate The Playground

- I can't read a book, because if I take my eyes off the kids for one second they will inevitably choose that moment to fall off the monkey bars and break an arm.
- I can't run off to the cafe to grab a coffee, because if I leave the playground for five minutes my kids will inevitably choose that moment to be abducted.
- I can't engage in small talk with the woman sitting next to me, because I will have to feign interest in her kids (who are no doubt perfectly behaved and scarily intelligent) and admiration for her parenting skills (which are no doubt superlative). Oh, and I will have to pretend to love the playground.
- The seats in the playground are hard, and they make my bottom ache and go numb.
- The seats in the playground are often covered in bird poo, which gets on my jeans.
- The seats in the playground are often sticky, which is just gross.
- Toddler will want me to push her on the swings, which is fine for the first ten minutes, but not so great for the next three hours.
- Little Man and Pinkela will want me to go on the swings with them. This isn't fine at all, and makes me hideously nauseous.
- Toddler will want me to go on the slide with her. Given that I am 102, this hurts my back.
- My kids will inevitably want something to eat. No matter what I have packed for them, no matter how much effort and preparation has gone into it, they won't want that. They will want what that other kid is eating. No, not that kid. The one over there.
- My kids will inevitably want ice-creams from the ice-cream van. The ice-creams will cost approximately fifteen pounds each, and the kids will discard them after a few licks and run back to the swings. So I'll end up eating three ice-creams on my

*own which will make me feel extremely ill, especially after that episode on the swings.*

- *My kids will need to go to the toilet, but there will not be a toilet for miles. When I tell Little Man to discreetly do a wee behind a tree, I will discover that he actually wants to do a poo. NOW.*

- *On the rare occasions when there is a toilet, it will have no seat, no toilet paper, and only half a door. I will be forced to hold Toddler in place on the bowl while jamming the door shut with my foot and wiping her bottom with a tiny piece of used tissue I found in my bag. This will make me want to go home and have a shower.*

# It's My (Child's) Party and I'll Cry If I Want To

$K$ ids' birthday parties aren't such a big deal. I mean, sure they take a bit of preparation and thought, and sure they are hard work on the day, but when you think about it, there's really not a lot at stake. Just, you know, your child's *happiness*.

Throwing birthday parties for my children is a bit like sitting for school exams, except that it's my fun quotient that's being examined, and I'm being assessed by much younger people. And with two kids whose birthdays fall in the same week in the same month, I find myself dreading that month for the entire year.

There is all the work that goes into the party beforehand: deciding on a 'theme', figuring out who to invite (just five close friends or the entire class?), buying the produce, booking the entertainment (or making it yourself), sending out invitations, and calling the 90 per cent of mothers who fail to RSVP. And then there is the day itself. The fact is, you will never, *ever* work as hard in your life as during the two hours of your child's birthday party, unless, of course, it is being held at a party venue, in which case you'll sit down with a glass of wine and toast to the fact that you and your child have survived another year.

No matter how much preparation you do, there are 100 different minor calamities (and a few major ones) that can go wrong at a child's birthday party. And inevitably, one or two of them actually do. Which is a shame, because at the end of the day all the birthday child really wants is to see their friends, get some presents, and eat some cake.

## Birthday Blues

- ♟ *I spend hours making clever invitations with photos and a poem, even though I know full well the parent will receive the invitation, mark the date in their diary, and throw the invite in the bin.*

- ♟ *I spend hours sourcing clever take-home gifts for each child and make my own lolly bags. Chances are the parents will eat the lollies, and the kids will throw their gifts in the bin, but it's one of those things you have to do.*

- ♟ *I put orange slices and carrot sticks next to the chips and chocolate on the table, to show the other parents how committed I am to healthy living. Even the other parents see how absurd and futile my efforts are.*

- ♟ *I make a pass-the-parcel with little gifts inside each layer. Some kids smile with barely concealed disappointment, some cry that they want the other prize, and some express their disappointment rather more vigorously by throwing the gift at another child's head.*

- ♟ *I make signs telling the kids which areas of the house they cannot enter. If the kids can read, they're certainly not doing it today.*

- ♟ *One child turns up with his three rowdy siblings in tow. 'You don't mind?' asks his mother, tucking into a chocolate crackle.*

🐻 *The kids ignore the games that I have carefully laid out, and end up bouncing with tremendous enthusiasm on my freshly made bed.*

🐻 *Pinkela has a fight with her best friend in the middle of the party.*

🐻 *Pinkela gets completely overwhelmed and retreats to her room in the middle of the party.*

🐻 *Pinkela cries and tells me that this party 'isn't nearly as good as Amy's Build-a-Bear party'.*

🐻 *Toddler is terrified of the clown and runs back screaming into the house.*

🐻 *I spend hours and hours making a beautiful cake for Pinkela with her name spelled out in lollies on the top. Pinkela looks briefly at the cake, sees chocolate, blows out the candles, and eats. Nobody notices the cake.*

🐻 *I realise I have forgotten to accommodate the children with 'special dietary requirements', and send The Architect out urgently to buy gluten- and dairy-free biscuits. The Architect misses the cutting of the cake, and the kids don't eat the biscuits anyway.*

🐻 *Pinkela turns up her nose as she opens her gifts in front of the assembled guests and parents. 'I don't much like this present,' she says. I decide it's time for the party to end.*

# Extreme Quality Time

The only things more challenging than birthday parties are school holidays. Sadly, they also last approximately 250 times longer.

The problem with school holidays is that a) my kids have a break from school but I don't have a break from work, and b) my kids have a break from school.

Now, school holidays have numerous advantages (using 'numerous' in the sense of 'very few'). I don't have to wash school uniforms and I don't have to make school lunches. (Of course, I still have to wash clothes, and I still have to make meals, but at least I don't have to put the meals in boxes.) And, of course, I get to spend Extreme Quality Time with my kids, but quite frankly two days of quality time each weekend and seventeen and a half hours each weekday are more than enough for me.

My kids, you see, aren't all that good at entertaining themselves. Toddler can occupy herself for very brief periods of time (during which there is massive destruction of property, massive consumption of inedibles, and the occasional wee in her pants), but then she insists on sitting on my knee for hours and hours, whether I am working at the computer, doing the laundry, or standing at the stove cooking dinner.

Pinkela doesn't require much attention, but this is due to a severe addiction to TV, rather than to any inner resources. She can park herself in front of the television for six to eight hours, which brings me some respite, but has unfortunate side effects, like headaches (for her), a dazed expression (her again), speaking in an American accent (still her), and major parental guilt (that one would be me).

Little Man, on the other hand, is unable to occupy himself for more than ... well ... at all, really. I can take him out for a whole day of exciting activities (for example, grocery shopping and getting a haircut) and within ten seconds of walking in the door he will be 'bored' again.

Now, obviously I don't give in to his constant pleas for entertainment. But neither can I completely ignore them. It's impossible, when his face is pressed against mine yelling, 'MUM, I'M BORED!', especially when I am attempting to go to the toilet.

So inevitably, I spend the days of the school holidays desperately trying to think of things for my kids to do. In particular, I look for activities that allow me to extract myself from my children's vice-like grips and get some work done. Or do a wee.

## What We Did On Our Holidays

**Day One:** *Went to the beach. Going to the beach is always so relaxing. I love balancing my own body weight in towels, beach toys, sunscreen, food and a small child, while trudging through sand with sweat trickling down my back. I love trying to keep track of all three children on long, crowded stretches of beach next to treacherous waves. I love schlepping back to the car two hours later, hot, sticky and tired, leaving enough sand in my car to create a small desert nation. And I am not at all traumatised by losing Pinkela* on the beach for an hour, only to find her sitting on a blanket with someone else's family. That just added to the excitement.

**Day Two:** *Went bowling. Bowling is a marvellous school holiday activity. I got to drive to the bowling alley, don shoes that had been worn by 750 other people, and have approximately thirty minutes of fun, all for the bargain price of around £70. Oh, and then I was able to give my kids dozens of coins for the games machines in the arcade, so that they could win fabulous prizes, such as minuscule plastic toys that fell apart by the time we got back to the car.*

**Day Three:** *Made a cake. This was a very pleasing way to while away a holiday morning. The kids' interest peaked at the pouring and stirring of ingredients, diminished somewhat at the transfer of the mixture to the pan, perked up again at the licking of the bowl, then fell off altogether at the washing-up. By the time the cake came out of the oven, everyone was so sick of the bloody thing that no one wanted to eat it. So I managed to entertain the family for about ten minutes, wash up for forty-five, and be left with an entire cake which I alone would binge on for the next five days.*

**Day Four:** *Did craft activities. This was also enormous fun. I spent twenty minutes laying out paper, stickers, scissors, paste and crayons, only to find the kids wandering off after five minutes to return to the TV. Without tidying up.*

**Day Five:** *Went to the movies. We left Toddler at Nana's, paid an exorbitant sum of money for three movie tickets, paid almost as much money again for popcorn and drinks, and sat down in a darkened room to watch some animated creation that would soon be on TV for free. As I fell asleep approximately three minutes after* *the previews began, and woke only when the lights went back on, it was possibly the most expensive nap I have ever had.*

**Day Six:** *Played games. Let me state for the record: I hate playing games. Though I love my children deeply, playing a board game with them is my idea of hell. However, after watching TV, going to the park, reading, and making a playhouse, we were still left with hours to go till bedtime. So we played Connect Four, at which I am useless, Scrabble, at which I am also useless ('Mum, you're a writer, how come you're so bad at this?' 'Because I'm USELESS, son. Okay?') and Monopoly, at which I am not so much useless as my son is ruthless. (Actually, I suspect he steals from the bank, but as I am always the banker, it is probably more my fault than his.) All in all, it was an ego-crushing experience.*

**Day Seven:** *Visited friends. This involved going to someone else's home and relaxing as the kids played together, trashed the house and emptied the kitchen of food. It also involved stopping on the way to pick up a peace offering (cake, alcohol, chocolate) to offset the damage inevitably done to furniture, floor, fridge and psyche.*

**Day Eight:** *Friends visited us. This was similar to the above, but much, much worse, as I was the one sustaining the damage. And let me tell you, the offering of cake, alcohol and chocolate were but small compensations for the four hours of cleaning that followed. What were they thinking?*

**Day Nine:** *Took the kids bike riding. This was tremendously enjoyable, and extremely good exercise, particularly when the kids took off really fast on their bikes and I lost sight of them and had to run panic-stricken at full pelt while pushing a very heavy toddler in a* *very heavy pram. Of course, once I found them, happily chatting together on a grassy knoll, it was all worthwhile. Not.*

**Day Ten:** *Went on an excursion. Little Man was pushing for a theme park, Pinkela was hoping to feed the ducks, and Toddler wanted to go 'to the moon'. I, however, had the deciding vote (and the moon wasn't practical, anyway). So off we trooped to our local shopping centre. We started with the supermarket, moved on to the fruit shop, had a quick detour to the butcher, and culminated our adventure with an exciting visit to the doctor's surgery. It may not have been fun, it may not have been educational, but at least we ended up with food.*

**Day Eleven:** *Tried to convince the kids that sorting laundry is an excellent holiday activity. This failed.*

**Day Twelve:** *Tried to convince the kids to run around the garden to wear themselves out. This failed.*

**Day Thirteen:** *Actually paid the kids to run around the garden to wear themselves out. This worked.*

**Day Fourteen:** *Watched TV all day and counted down the minutes till school started.*

# Better Be Worth It

*O*ne option for the school holidays is travel, provided you have the means, the time off from work, and, of course, the stamina. Travelling with kids can be extremely rewarding, but it inevitably involves some challenges.

For a start, there is the packing. To get a sense of packing for the average holiday with children, think of packing for a trip to the beach, multiply it by 100, and add several extra bottles of sunscreen. And it is impossible to avoid either overpacking, underpacking or packing like a lunatic.

I fall into the packing-like-a-lunatic category. On a recent seven-day holiday with friends, I brought along two varieties of toothpaste, about 10,000 nappies, every children's DVD ever made, 150 outfits for Toddler, five packets of biscuits, and two foam visors for the older kids to decorate (don't even ask). I did, however, neglect to pack such minor essentials as pyjamas for my daughter, a jacket for my son, long-sleeved tops for me, and chocolate. So as evening fell, we huddled frozen in front of the television, watching *Shrek* on DVD, trying to warm ourselves by burning nappies as I satisfied my chocolate cravings with choc-flavoured wafer biscuits.

Still, at least that holiday didn't involve plane travel. Becoming airborne with small children requires enormous fortitude. You can either balance your baby on your lap, and be unable to move for three hours after she falls asleep on your knee, or tuck her into an aeroplane fold-out cot – the perfect size for a baby, provided she doesn't come complete with limbs and a head. Then you can experience the delights of changing a nappy in an aeroplane toilet, especially when turbulence hits at the exact moment you have removed the nappy from her bum. And watch your kids' reactions to their special aeroplane meals, as they turn up their noses at the reheated flabby fries and gorge on chocolate cookies till they vomit. Then force your kids to sit still for six hours; not a problem at all, if the person in the seat directly in front doesn't mind being kicked in the back, and the person behind enjoys empty orange juice containers being flung at his head.

Of course, the destination is worth the journey. Or is it? After all, travelling with kids isn't like travelling alone, for the simple reason that you bring your parenting duties with you.

We've had wonderful holidays with the kids. There are memories that we will all carry with us forever – memories of fire-lighting ceremonies in Fiji with Little Man dressed in a grass skirt, memories of building sandcastles at twilight on the beach in Thailand, memories of snowball fights on the ski slopes of Perisher. But other somewhat less idyllic moments also spring to mind. Pinkela burning with fever for four days in a foreign country. Toddler waking me up several times a night, unable to sleep soundly in an unfamiliar bed. And Little Man being cranky and unsettled for days at a time in a new environment.

Moving your family and possessions to another destination doesn't necessarily constitute a holiday. Sometimes it's just your ordinary life in a different location. And on those occasions, it can be easier to stay home.

## Leaving Home

♀ You pay thousands of pounds for a resort with a kids' club, so that you can spend some quality time by the pool with your spouse (using 'spouse' in its lesser known sense of 'strawberry daiquiri'). Your kids try it out for an hour on the first day, say, 'We don't like kids' club,' then cling to your sides like little monkeys for the rest of the trip.

♀ You look for the best place to put the portacot in the hotel room so that Toddler gets peace and quiet. As there is no peace and quiet to be had, she ends up sleeping in the bathroom.

♀ You spend hours every day trying to find food on the restaurant menu for your children to eat. While the breakfast buffet is great (after all, who doesn't like Coco Pops?), the day goes gastronomically downhill from then on. The juice tastes 'funny'. The cheese tastes 'funny'. The tomato sauce tastes 'funny'. The hot dogs taste 'funny'. The burger doesn't taste like Mum's, and it doesn't taste like McDonald's (and even if it is McDonald's, it doesn't taste like the McDonald's at home). They do not make 'plain noodles'. They do not even understand 'plain noodles'. And it is fifteen quid for a children's meal, of which your child will eat three bites and discard the rest.

♀ If your room has pay TV, your child will wish to stay inside all day watching TV, even though you've paid a fortune for this lovely resort.

♀ If your room doesn't have pay TV, your child will complain.

♀ Away from your home routine, your toddler will become feral. Trying to replicate your home routine is a complete waste of energy.

♀ Your husband will expect to have sex every night (and, scarily, some mornings). He does not understand that this is a HOLIDAY from ALL duties.

♀ *Your children will still wake you up early. But you've been up even later than at home because your husband expects you to have SEX EVERY NIGHT.*

♀ *In the chaos of trying to pack for five people, you will forget your own swimsuit, and be forced to wear a jewelled turquoise number from the gift shop for the duration of your stay.*

♀ *In the chaos of trying to pack for five people, you will forget your deodorant, and be forced to buy a can for £12.99 from the boutique.*

♀ *In the chaos of trying to pack for five people, you forget your essential medication, and spend the first day of your holiday frantically calling doctors and visiting local pharmacies in town.*

♀ *In the chaos of trying to pack for five people, you forget to pack your toddler's precious blanky, and spend the first day of your holiday frantically searching for a replacement.*

♀ *You run out of nappies after four days and are forced to buy more at the gift shop at outrageous cost. You inform your toddler that she is only allowed to poo once a day, as the wildly expensive nappies work out to be £2.99 per poo.*

♀ *Inevitably it will rain for at least two days of the trip. Being at home in the rain is annoying enough. Being on holidays in the rain is like being trapped in a cage with three angry tigers. There are only so many games of Connect Four and Monopoly one can throw at them before they eventually turn on you and chew your leg off.*

# Doing the Group Thing

*A*nother option for school holidays is to share the burden with friends, through the phenomenon known as the 'group holiday'.

My family has had many experiences involving the group holiday, including a mammoth, seven-night, seven-family coastal adventure. And when I say seven families, I don't mean a sedate group of ten or so adults and a dozen kids. I mean a wild, rumbling, rowdy crowd of fourteen adults, seventeen children, and three babies under the age of two. The experience was enlightening, and, for the most part, highly enjoyable. It was also chaotic, loud, exhausting, frenzied, and did I mention chaotic?

What's more, the holiday left us with virtually no privacy. I regularly woke in the mornings (early, I might add) to the sound of six or seven children playing in our cabin, rummaging through our fridge, and using our toilet. And upon leaving our cabin, I was regularly confronted with the vision of my friends' husbands in their unshaven, semi-dressed morning glory (which was sometimes a little too … er … *intense* to deal with before I'd had my coffee).

Most worrying, however, was that every instance of slight marital discord was on public display for more than thirty pairs of curious eyes. We had to listen to the fighting of the other couples, and they had to listen to ours. What's worse, we had to notice that the other couples seemed to argue far less frequently than we did.

There were also other issues to contend with. Parenting, for example. Though I was already aware that not everybody has the same parenting style as me (my particular parenting style being defined as 'the attempt to cling to sanity when everybody around me is losing theirs'), I didn't expect this to pose a problem. However, when kids from other families were still running around three hours after my kids' usual bedtime, or when my kids cried, 'Jack ate Coco Pops for dinner, why can't we?' or, 'Chloe got the souvenir drink bottle from the gift shop, can I have one, too?', it got rather more tricky.

Discipline, too, was potentially contentious. While I welcome any other adult to discipline my kids (hey, they can use all the reprimanding they can get), I'm aware that not every parent feels the same about their own kids. So on the holiday I erred on the side of caution. Any child who behaved badly in my presence was given one gentle warning, then escorted back to the care of their parents. This was a satisfying and effective solution when the child belonged to someone else. Not surprisingly, however, it was rather less satisfying when the child belonged to me. (And frequently, the child did belong to me.)

Still, I'd certainly go on a group holiday again. Only next time, I'll pack several large boxes of Coco Pops.

And travel with men who look good in their pyjamas.

# A Day(trip) in the Life

*I*f a full-blown holiday is too much trouble, a daytrip can be an inexpensive, restorative and simple solution. Or at least it used to be, back in the days before children. The Architect and I would hop into the car, turn on the radio and relax as we drove through the city to the countryside, stopping for leisurely lunches and Devonshire teas along the way. We had some of our best conversations in the car. And when we didn't want to speak we had quiet. Blissful, brain-soothing quiet.

Not anymore.

Our daytrip experiences have changed somewhat since the arrival of our children (and when I say 'somewhat', I mean 'considerably' and 'for the worse'). Children and cars do not go well together. You see, confining children to a small space – even if it is in motion – with no possibility of running, jumping, raiding the fridge or getting wet can be fraught with danger. If there is no fun to be found easily on hand, then there certainly will be some trouble.

Hopefully in the near future someone will invent teleportation, so that mums can transport their offspring to another location without ever having to move them from the couch. In the meantime, we must get there by car. And, while a car trip is far preferable to walking with three children for forty miles, or travelling by horse and cart, it definitely has its challenges.

## *Are We Nearly There?*

🥿 *Every car journey begins with the requisite Packing of Provisions. No longer can my husband and I jump into the car spontaneously and take off. Now, we must pack for every possible contingency. Wipes in case of spills. Drinks in case of thirst. Snacks in case of hunger (several options, as God forbid the kids want that, and I only have this). Nappies in case of poo. Toys in case of boredom. And composure in case of dramas. Because there will be some.*

🥿 *Since my car doubles as a storage facility, I must empty several tonnes of detritus onto the garage floor before we can all fit into the vehicle. Clothes, foodstuffs, schoolwork, hairbrushes, newspapers, and – inexplicably – my mouthguard are tossed haphazardly out the door and we pile in.*

🥿 *Toddler insists on climbing into her car seat herself. This takes approximately three false starts and sixteen minutes, until she gives up and allows me to place her there myself.*

🥿 *As I attempt to herd the kids into their seats, they argue about who sits in the front, who sits in the back, and who gets to hold Mum's phone.*

🥿 *As I place my hands on the steering wheel, I notice that it is sticky. The cause of the stickiness is unknown. I feel slightly queasy.*

🥿 *As I turn on the radio, the children argue about what station we will listen to. The dispute cannot be resolved so we agree to just listen to them arguing.*

🥿 *As we leave the garage, the kids ask, 'Are we nearly there?' They ask the same question every seven minutes for the duration of the trip.*

👠 As we leave our street, my son announces that he is hungry.

👠 As we leave our suburb, my daughter announces that she has to wee.

👠 As we enter the freeway, Toddler announces that she has to poo.

👠 I struggle to maintain concentration while driving on a wet freeway as my three children argue in the back seat.

👠 I struggle even harder to maintain concentration while driving on a wet freeway as my kids insist I 'go faster to beat all the other cars'.

👠 I struggle exceedingly to maintain concentration while driving on a wet freeway as my kids poke me in the back.

👠 So desperate am I to get to my destination that I fail to notice my petrol gauge is on nearly empty.

👠 We search desperately for a service station in the middle of nowhere in the pouring rain as my petrol gauge flashes red. I tell the kids it is an adventure. They roll their eyes and return to arguing.

## Keeping House

# God Grant Me a Housekeeper

*I* resent housework. It chips away at my morale and eats away my soul. I do not understand why the desire to procreate and raise citizens of the world should, in practical terms, mean washing dozens of underpants and cleaning yoghurt off the walls. No one tells you that this is what your life will become – a daily routine of laundry, cleaning, sweeping and washing. Which is why, if I could be granted one wish in my life, I'd ask for a full-time housekeeper.

Oh okay, *okay*, I'd ask for health and happiness for my loved ones. Of course. But let me tell you, I think there'd be a lot better chance of guaranteeing health and happiness for my loved ones if I had a full-time housekeeper. After all, a happy, relaxed mummy makes for a happy, relaxed child. And a happy, relaxed wife makes for a happy, relaxed hubby. With a lot more opportunities for sex, too.

I need a housekeeper. Badly. I have three kids, a house, and a part-time job, and I do not recall one single day in the past eleven years when I have gone to bed knowing I have finished everything I needed to do.

This is not just because I am a little disorganised and waste several precious hours every week searching for my keys (which often turn up on the inside of my locked house). It is because on any given day I have about forty-three minutes in which to complete the housework. And in those forty-three minutes, Toddler needs entertaining, the shopping needs unpacking, the laundry needs folding, the dishwasher needs emptying, the floor needs sweeping, the beds need changing, the shirts need ironing, and the dinner needs cooking (or at least picking up from the local chicken shop).

And, sadly, forty-three minutes is around three hours too little time.

So as a busy working mother, I need to prioritise my tasks. This means that I frequently have to make some tough decisions. Do I shave my legs or wash my hair? Do I pay the bills, or earn some money so that I can do so? Do I make the beds, or pick the toys up from the floor? Do I ensure my kids have done their homework, or that they are fed, bathed and clothed?

The answer is: I don't know. So I do what I always do in this situation – start running around anxiously in circles in the kitchen feeling overwhelmed by my life, before sitting down with a jar of Nutella and a spoon and dreaming longingly of a housekeeper.

Now I wouldn't want my housekeeper to live at home with us; God knows I wouldn't want to expose her to some of the shenanigans that go on around here. I'd just want her to arrive at about seven in the morning, and stay till eight or nine at night. Seven days a week. Three hundred and sixty-five days of the year. Of course, I wouldn't expect her to actually work full-time, and she could certainly take an afternoon off once a week, as long as she'd made the school lunches for the following day and laid out the clean uniforms. No doubt we could manage alone on a Sunday evening. We get takeaway on Sunday nights, anyway.

## What I Do All Day

♀ *I clean the dishes, sweep the floors and change the sheets, and within an hour or a day or a week there are more dishes, more dirt and more sheets to wash.*

♀ *I do the laundry day after day after day, often two or three times a day. With three kids, four beds, and around seventeen towels on each bathroom floor, this is a lot of laundry. Understandably, clothes at the bottom of the pile can get trapped in the basket for some days, even weeks. The Architect refers to the laundry basket as 'The Place My Shirts Go to Die', but as I don't feel a sense of compassion towards clothing, this doesn't bother me.*

♀ *Every now and then I iron my husband's shirts. I say 'now and then', because – although his shirts need ironing every day – I do not get round to them for a month or so. It's not that I hate ironing, it's just that there are so many other, less challenging things to do. You know, like scrubbing the oven, or doing my income tax return. It is only when my husband leaves for work wearing a suit, a tie, and an M&S T-shirt that I haul out the ironing board and do it. And on a good day, I'll only destroy one shirt. Or maybe two.*

♀ *I buy food and grocery items constantly. And it is a constant source of astonishment to me that children who seem to eat little more than cheese sandwiches and Kit Kats can get through such trolley loads of food. As for the truckloads of toilet paper, rolls and rolls of cling film, and dozens upon dozens of disposable plastic containers that never seem to have matching lids after they have been carefully stored away in the cupboard ...*

*well ... sometimes I wonder whether I have an extra family of five living somewhere in my pantry. And if I do, I really wish they'd stop stealing the last slice of bread.*

♀ *I clean out Spunky the rabbit's cage. I deeply resent this task as I have cleaned up enough of my human children's poo to last a lifetime. Besides, cleaning the cage is supposed to be the kids' job. They promised me that they would do it every week. And no, I can't believe I fell for their lies, either.*

♀ *I pay the bills on occasion. It is my delegated responsibility to pay bills in my household, and I take my duties seriously. I allow the bills to stack up on my desk, then watch with tremendous interest as they multiply exponentially in an extremely short period of time, like some kind of deadly bacteria in a laboratory. And then when the pile is terrifyingly large, I take a deep breath and work my way through it. Sometimes I even do it without breaking into a cold sweat. Okay, not really. But I'm hoping to one day.*

♀ *I pay The Architect's parking fines. This requires a category of its own as it is such a frequent and burdensome task. I pay each fine at the last possible moment, flirting every time with the tantalising possibility of allowing him to go to jail instead. Inevitably, though, I pay the fine, as I figure the financial consequences of him being imprisoned would be fairly aggravating – not to mention having to schlep the kids to visit him in jail every other weekend.*

♀ *I buy the kids their clothes, shoes, books, sporting equipment, stationery, labels, creams, lotions, toys, lunch boxes, drink bottles, hats, calculators, pencil cases, socks, undies, swimsuits, bedding, bags, towels, Game Boys, and every other type of paraphernalia a child in the western world requires to get through the day. And just when I think I've got them everything they need, they lose something, or bring home another textbook list, or grow, and I have to go running to the shops again.*

♀ *I maintain my car in perfect condition. Okay, so that's not exactly true. I am supposed to maintain my car in perfect condition. But something has to give, and keeping my car regularly serviced has had to fall by the wayside. Of course, I put petrol in my car reasonably regularly. I have learned that when the little red light comes on, the car will actually stop working if I don't fill up the tank. But the servicing thing is a bit harder to manage. How can I do without a car for two or three days? How can I get my kids to their schools, without any vehicle, all before nine a.m.? By air? Which is why it seems to me to be more time effective just to wear this vehicle into the ground, and when it breaks down completely, buy another. Strangely, however, my husband doesn't agree. But then he's not the one who has to fly the kids to school.*

♀ *I cook for my family. I cook almost every day. Of course, I use the term 'cook' fairly liberally. I use it to refer not only to meals prepared in a pot or oven, but also to two-minute noodles (especially if I use the flavour sachet), taco kits (where I have to brown the meat), microwaved leftovers (particularly ones which need to be defrosted), and the omnipresent frankfurter. Cheese on toast is not 'cooked', although a double-sided toastie is. And cereal is most definitely not cooked, but if it's followed up with a glass of milk and some grapes, then it is a perfectly adequate (though still somewhat shameful) meal.*

♀ *I tidy. Endlessly. Okay, sporadically. But still.*

# Domestic Goddess... Not

*M*y other problem with housework is that I am just not very good at it. It is sad but true: I am lousy at keeping house. Not only am I not a Domestic Goddess, I wouldn't even qualify for High Priestess, let alone Minor Deity. And this is something I was not prepared for when I had children. I just assumed I would intuitively know how to keep an impeccable home. No one warned me that it doesn't happen instinctively for everyone – that creating life in one's womb does not guarantee skills in time management, ironing, stain removal or cleaning delicate glass without streaks.

It's not that I don't put effort into the housework. I do. I spend approximately one hour out of every three performing some kind of household activity. It's just that the results aren't as perfect as I would hope them to be (using 'perfect' in the sense of 'moderately effective'). In fact, more often than not I create more problems than I solve. Which means I should probably give up trying to do housework.

Or move my family into a hotel.

## *Housekeeping Disasters*

♀ When washing my floors, I am unable to remove the dirt, no matter how much water I use. It just swirls in all different directions around my house.

♀ When spot-cleaning my carpet, I am unable to remove the small, discrete stains. I just transform them into massive circles of grey.

♀ I regularly forget to hold on to my glassware and crockery when transporting them to the cupboards. Consequently, we have about three plates and four bowls between the five of us.

♀ I regularly miss the tissues that find their way into the wash, leaving the entire family looking like we are covered in dandruff. This doesn't bother my kids, who think it looks like snow, but it certainly doesn't please my husband.

♀ I regularly drop items of clothing into the bucket of whites soaking in bleach, causing an interesting tie-dyed effect. I deal with this situation by proudly informing my daughter that I have made her 'something very special'. Sadly, this does not work on my son or husband.

♀ I regularly cause the disintegration of items of white clothing by leaving them soaking in bleach for several weeks. This has no possible solution.

♀ I regularly must convince my husband that the huge iron-shaped brown patches on his shirts must be the result of coffee stains, as they were definitely not there when I was finished with them. This is despite the fact that he doesn't drink coffee. Oh, and that coffee tends not to fall in iron-shaped patches, anyway.

♀ I regularly discover small objects banging around in the washing machine. According to the repairman, this is not ideal for its optimal performance.

♀ *I place my treasured woollen garments tenderly in the laundry basket to await handwashing. They stay there until they are accidentally shoved in the machine amid a pile of towels, to emerge twenty minutes later as dolly clothes.*

♀ *I carefully wash my few remaining woollen items by hand. After drying, they are destroyed in a tragic, overenthusiastic de-pilling accident.*

♀ *At least one of each pair of socks seems to use our washing machine as a portal into an alternate universe, into which it escapes and is never heard from again. We currently have thirty-seven socks, none of which bear any resemblance whatsoever to each other.*

♀ *I begin any spring-cleaning project with tremendous enthusiasm, only to run out of steam just at the moment the furniture has been moved, the cupboards have been emptied, and the cleaning products have been strewn all over the floor.*

# I'll Die with a Sponge in My Hand

Mess is the enemy of the human mother, and the natural state of the human child. Children ooze mess. They breed the stuff. They scatter it in their wake, in the form of clothing, toys, books, bags, foodstuffs, leaves, homework, pencils, sand, wrappers, stickers, hairclips, blankets, cups, fingernails, tissues, and pretty much every other form of detritus created on this earth. And the mess produced by children grows at an exponential and fantastically speedy rate. It needs to be kept very tightly under control, or within hours it becomes virtually impossible to destroy without the help of a team of assistants, and several dozen rubbish bags.

Now, every mother knows that the only way to contain mess when you have children is to Clean Up As You Go Along. Toddler tips her bowl of cereal on the floor, The Architect throws his plate in the sink, Little Man drops his lunch box on the counter, Pinkela leaves her undies in the bathroom, and immediately, before the mess can take hold and begin multiplying, each item is picked up and put away.

Perfect theory. Makes absolute sense. But strangely, it is not so easy to execute. Take, for example, Toddler tipping her bowl of cereal on the floor. Well, she doesn't just get a great deal of

Weetabix on the floorboards; she also gets a great deal of it on herself. So then I have a choice. I can put Toddler aside and clean up the floor straightaway, but this leaves Toddler free to rub her sticky fingers all over herself and her chair, not to mention fling chunky bits of Weetabix all over the room. Or I can deal with Toddler first, and then return to clean up the mess on the floor. Of course, by the time I get to the mess, Toddler is just as likely to have begun a small fire in another part of the house, or emptied a cupboard, or scribbled on the walls, so it will be a while before I get to the congealed cereal. And besides, while all this is going on Little Man has left toothpaste on the sink, Pinkela has deposited nail clippings on the table, and The Architect has walked out the door leaving his dirty towels in the bath.

And it's only eight a.m.

This is the problem with mess. *All* mess. No matter how quickly I run to stamp it out, there is someone, somewhere, in another part of my home, who is working even harder to make some more. It doesn't end. It will never end. I will go on cleaning, for the rest of my life, until I die with a sponge in my hand.

Interestingly, this is something that many husbands do not understand. This is possibly because they work in an environment in which everyone is over the age of eighteen and cleans up after themselves, or where someone cleans up after the lot of them. Or it's possibly because they're just really insensitive. Either way, it's hugely annoying.

Still, there do exist some women who manage to achieve tidy homes at all times, despite having numerous children, and, occasionally, even a husband. Some of these women are called 'demented'. The others have excellent cleaners.

As for me, well, I can be found on any given day surrounded by a splendid assortment of mess of all different shapes, sizes and sources.

## Welcome to My Home. Look Around and You Will Find...

❧ A bottle of very average cabernet sauvignon sitting on the kitchen table. The poor quality of the wine does not in the slightest detract from its alcoholic potency, which is why, despite being so crap, it is now nearly empty.

❧ The newspapers from the previous weekend. Out of the twelve or so sections, I have managed to read approximately one and a half stories.

❧ Pinkela's school homework, which was supposed to be with her at school. This does not reflect kindly on my parenting skills.

❧ A chair. Covered in marker pen. This does not reflect kindly on my disciplinary skills.

❧ A Paint-With-Water book. This is my favourite toy. It means that Toddler can paint with water to create colours, then do it again when the water dries. Sadly, it is not Toddler's favourite toy. She prefers marker pen.

❧ Several types of cleaning spray, with which I've tried to remove the marker pen. None of them worked.

❧ A bath towel I've forgotten to put into the wash. It is covered in pumpkin soup. I have no idea why.

❧ A Dairylea Dunkers label. I can't recall anyone eating a Dairylea Dunkers in our home for at least a month.

❧ A pile of bills, some due three weeks ago.

❧ A potty, completely redundant. Toddler uses it as a hat.

❧ Pinkela's Work Samples Folder from the previous term at school, including her symmetrical drawing of a face, complete with her description of why she enjoyed that particular exercise: 'Drawing a symmetrical face is fun because I love drawing symmetrical faces. It's fun!'

❧ A broken label maker.

❧ A broken phone.

🥿 *A broken watch.*

🥿 *Several dirty tea towels, placed optimistically at the top of the stairs for imminent transportation to the laundry basket. They have been there for three days.*

🥿 *Several shirts awaiting ironing, placed optimistically next to the ironing board. They have been there for a week.*

🥿 *A tube of hand cream from 1994.*

🥿 *The breakfast dishes. From yesterday.*

🥿 *Several nappies (mostly clean).*

🥿 *My keys. At least I hope you will find them. I certainly can't.*

# Darwinian Household Management

*I*n my early days as a parent I was highly organised. Meticulous, even. Toys were put straight back on the shelves as soon as they were used, together with all of their pieces. (I know! Can you imagine?) Items of clothing were hung straight back on their hangers. Post was opened, attended to, and filed away. Shopping was unpacked without delay. Even photographs were sorted and placed into albums within a week of being printed.

Of course, this was back when I had had only one child, who was immobile and couldn't make a mess. Once Little Man could actually walk, things became somewhat less ordered. When Pinkela, and then Toddler, arrived, I gave up all semblance of trying to maintain control. And, having gone back to part-time work while still being a mother (because, as I've discovered, you can't actually resign from one job simply because you take on another), I have accepted the chaos that is my life.

Now I work according to the Darwinian principle of household management. Whatever survives in my home, survives. And whatever doesn't, must go by the wayside. It is survival of the fittest. And so far, it is working very well.

## Survival of the Fittest

♀ I have long since stopped watering our plants. If they can't live without water, they will die, and will be replaced by whatever hardy plant (or, ahem, weed) sprouts in their absence. This system has worked extremely well, and we now have a flourishing garden. Of course, it is largely dominated by mushrooms – the yucky kind that comes from rain, not the tasty kind you put in salads – but at least it is thriving.

♀ I no longer spend hours trying to recover each piece of a toy before putting it back in the cupboard. Whatever survives, survives. And if Toddler never knows the joy of completing a puzzle because a piece is missing from each box, then she will grow stronger for trying (and trying, and trying...).

♀ If a toy breaks, it breaks. It does not get replaced, because it will just break again. And it does not get fixed, because if it is so ridiculously fragile then it simply does not deserve to be fixed. Besides, the kids generally don't notice anyway. They'd be just as happy to play with the box.

♀ When shopping for computers and phones, I always let Toddler play with any item we are thinking of purchasing. If the salesman comes running and yells, 'Stop! She'll break it!', then clearly it is far too delicate to have in our home.

♀ I don't bother printing our photographs anymore. I figure it's just as easy – no, easier – to view them on a screen as in an album. And if the photos ever get accidentally wiped, well, there is always memory to sustain us.

♀ Clothes do not get 'darned'. I do not darn. To be honest, I'm not even sure what darning is. Clothes are worn until they fall apart, and then they are thrown into the bin.

♀ I buy hardy clothes that can withstand the washing machine. If they get shrunk or torn, then they shall be worn as such. This is

*why I favour jeans, as they are virtually indestructible. Flimsy*
*cashmere cardigans? Not so much.*

♀ *I do not wash pillows that have become disgusting after exten-*
*sive contact with sweaty little heads, as this generally results in*
*a pillow with the texture of wet newspaper wrapped in fabric.*
*Far better, I have learned, just to buy another pillow.*

♀ *Foodstuffs must be able to survive being left in the car for hours*
*after I forget to unpack the shopping. For this reason, I very*
*rarely buy sushi.*

♀ *School lunches must be able to survive bruising, age, heat, and,*
*frequently, dropping on the floor. For this reason, my kids eat a*
*lot of Vegemite sandwiches.*

# Shop at Your Own Risk

*A*s a mother of three I need to go supermarket shopping. A lot. It seems that no matter how much I buy – and believe me, I buy a lot – I inevitably need more within forty-eight hours. Still, the experience itself is not unpleasant. There is nothing intrinsically wrong with walking up and down aisles looking at items then transferring them to your possession – even if those items do happen to be sponges, boxes of cereal and tinned spaghetti. Or at least, there wouldn't be anything wrong with it if I was alone. The problem, of course, is that I am not. Given that one of my kids is a toddler (and the others were toddlers at one stage – they all seem to start that way), I have to shop with her.

And this is not easy, I can assure you.

Now, I tried online shopping for a while, but it did not go well. For a start, I would forget things, all the time. If I am not actually walking down the aisles looking directly at all the items I need, I don't remember to buy them. (Come to think of it, even when I *am* looking directly at all the items I need, I don't always remember to buy them.)

Furthermore, I got tired of the ridiculous substitutions that the supermarket would make. No, Mr Supermarket Packer, when I ask for girls toddler nappies and you are out of stock, a packet of boys infant nappies will NOT suffice. Likewise, if I request ten plain beef sausages to feed my kids, twenty chilli beef sausages are *not* going to do the trick. And when I ask for a Cadbury's Fruit and Nut bar, and you give me *plain* ... well, our relationship is definitely over.

So off to the supermarket I trudge, bag over one shoulder, list clutched in my hand, and Toddler tucked under one arm.

Welcome to shopping hell.

## Shopping with Toddler: A Timeline

**9.00:** *We arrive at the supermarket and head for the trolleys. Clearly, trolley theft is a major issue in today's materialistic society, because I need to insert a pound coin into the trolley just to unleash it. Having only been to the supermarket about 50,000 times, I haven't remembered to bring a pound coin, so I must rush to the nearest shop to get change. Then, having only used a trolley about 50,000 times, I can't work out which slot to put the coin into, so I must ask the nearest capable-looking shopper (that is, anyone but me).*

**9.12:** *Toddler asks to sit in the trolley. Only after I get her in do I realise I've scored the trolley with the wonky front wheel, which is more difficult to manoeuvre than a space shuttle. Unfortunately, as I am just as incapable of retrieving my pound coin as I was to insert it, I am stuck with the trolley for the rest of my shopping expedition.*

**9.17:** *We choose vegetables. I notice that Toddler has shredded an entire lettuce onto the floor. I move the lettuce out of Toddler's reach. I notice that she is eating a telegraph cucumber with the plastic wrapper still on.*

**9.25:** *I realise I have forgotten my shopping list, which no doubt means I'll end up with even more olives, laksa paste, oregano, and felt tips, while forgetting minor essentials such as bread, milk, and toilet paper. Then again, it probably doesn't matter. Even when I do remember my list, I generally can't read it.*

**9.27:** *Toddler wants to get out of the trolley. I haul her out.*

**9.31:** *We choose bread. Toddler wants to eat a piece of bread. I open the bread and give her a slice. Toddler eats three bites and then starts shredding the rest of the bread onto the floor.*

**9.35:** *Toddler wants to get in the trolley. I haul her in.*

**9.42:** *We choose juice. Toddler wants some juice. I give her juice. She takes one sip and starts sprinkling the rest on herself.*

**9.43:** *Toddler wants to get out of the trolley. I haul her out.*

**9.51:** *Toddler sees chocolate. I tell her she is allowed to get a Kinder Surprise. She runs across the aisle. Someone bumps into my trolley. I lose sight of Toddler.*

**9.52:** *I spend fifteen panicked minutes running around the supermarket looking for Toddler. Eventually I find her in the care of an old lady in aisle thirteen. The lady clicks her tongue disapprovingly at me. I slink off in shame.*

**10.07:** *Toddler gets her Kinder Surprise. I choose yoghurt.*

**10.08:** *Toddler wants to get in the trolley. I haul her in.*

**10.09:** *Toddler eats her chocolate (using 'eat' in the sense of 'puts into her mouth via her entire body').*

**10.11:** *I run with Toddler to aisle five, pick up a packet of baby wipes, and clean her up as she yells for more chocolate.*

**10.13:** *We progress to the grocery items. I catch Toddler throwing the used wipes out of the trolley. An old lady clicks her tongue disapprovingly at me.*

**10.14:** *We choose some grocery items. Toddler tries to eat the washing powder. I do not let her. She begins crying.*

**10.15:** *I offer Toddler some biscuits. She beams and eats half a biscuit before delightedly crumbling the rest into the trolley.*

**10.20:** *Toddler spies a toy. It is a small, soft rattle for ages zero to four months. She will never use it in her life. I say no. Toddler screams. An old lady walks past and clicks her tongue disapprovingly. I put the toy in the trolley.*

**10.22:** *Toddler wants to get out of the trolley. I haul her out.*

**10.23:** *Toddler announces that she needs to do a poo. NOW. I leave the trolley, grab Toddler and the wipes, and rush to the nearest toilet. Sadly, I am too late.*

**10.31:** *Toddler and I return to the supermarket with my spirit crushed and Toddler gleefully naked from the waist down. An old lady walks past and clicks her tongue disapprovingly. I duck into aisle eight and grab the only pair of tracksuit pants available in a size two. They are blue with a motif of little trucks, bearing the words 'Boys rule'.*

**10.33:** *Toddler cries that she doesn't want to wear them. 'No kidding,' I say.*

**10.34:** *We finish our shopping at lightning pace. I run through the aisles, throwing in items haphazardly, as Toddler tries desperately to pluck the pants from her body.*

**10.41:** *Toddler cries that she wants to go home. 'YOU want to go home?' I ask.*

**10.42:** *We get in line for the cashier. 'Sorry, I'm closing after this customer,' she says.*

**10.43:** *We get in line for another cashier. 'Sorry, I'm just doing a home delivery, might take a while,' she says.*

**10.44:** *We get in line for another cashier. 'Sorry, I'm in training, please accept my apology in advance,' he says. I look desperately around. There is no other option. 'Okay,' I sigh.*

**10.45:** *The cashier picks up an item, cradles it in his hands, examines it, scans it carefully then places it tenderly in a bag. He* then repeats this for all 156 items. Toddler begins howling. 'I tired!' she wails.

**10.46:** 'Did you bring your own shopping bags?' the cashier asks. 'No,' I admit sheepishly. The old lady behind me clicks her tongue disapprovingly.

**11.15:** A mere twenty-nine minutes later, we are all done. I throw money at the cashier, shove a screaming Toddler into the trolley, and rush to the car park.

**11.17:** I arrive at the car park. The car has been stolen. Either that, or I have not the faintest idea where it is parked.

**11.35:** Eighteen minutes later, we are in the car. I drive home rapidly, worried about the food defrosting in the boot.

**11.50:** I unload Toddler, take her inside, and put her into her cot. I then sit down at the computer and do some work.

**3.15:** With a sinking feeling, I remember the shopping in the car.

# Supermarket Etiquette

*I*t is not just the invigorating presence of Toddler that makes shopping less than ideal. There is also the annoying presence of Other People. Now, Other People are not always deliberately rude or unkind. Often they are simply unaware of the implicit rules of engagement that lend order to the store, and allow customers and cashiers to interact with dignity and decorum.

So I have decided to openly articulate these unspoken rules. They could be posted at every supermarket entrance, along with the signs saying 'We retain the right to search bags' and 'Smile! You're on security camera!' Read before you enter, and leave without incident.

Because I've got a trolley in my hands, and it's loaded with a crazy toddler, and you don't want to mess with me.

## An Open Letter to My Local Supermarket

**Dear Customers of My Distant Acquaintance,**

*When I bump into you, please pretend not to notice the Rescue Remedy, condoms, pregnancy testing kits, feminine hygiene products, and five extra-large jars of Nutella in my trolley. In return, I will happily ignore the lubricant, Horny Goat Weed, Hamburger Helper, and seven large packets of chips in yours.*

**Dear Kindly Older Person,**

*Please refrain from commenting on how loud my child is with remarks, such as, 'Ooh, she's got a good set of lungs on her!' and, 'Well, she certainly knows how to make herself heard!' Yes, I know my child is loud. I live with her. I was there when she came out of my tummy and the midwife said, 'That's the loudest cry I've ever heard!' So when you comment on it, it doesn't make me warm to you. It just makes me want to smack you.*

**Dear Unkindly Older Person,**

*Please feel free to sigh and roll your eyes at my child. Rest assured, though, that it will not make her any quieter. It will, however, make me much more determined to take my time.*

**Dear Well-meaning Person of Questionable Standards of Hygiene,**

*No, I'm sorry, but it is not okay to touch my toddler without my permission. And no, it is definitely not okay for you to feed her lollies out of your own unhygienic pocket. Ugh.*

**Dear Married Couple Shopping Together,**

*No, it is not acceptable to stand guard at two check-outs to see 'which is free first'. I mean, seriously.*

**Dear Cashier,**

*If my toddler steals a chocolate from the shelf directly in her line of sight at the check-out, which was placed there by your bosses to force me into a purchase I had no intention of making by unfairly manipulating my child, then no, I am not going to pay for it.*

**Dear Customer in Front of Me at the Check-out,**

*No, it is not acceptable to request a price check on an article worth* less than two quid. I would rather give you the money for the stupid set of scourers than wait eight minutes for you to learn that the price is, indeed, £1.29, and not £1.19 as you insisted.

### Dear Customers Waiting Behind Me at the Check-out,
If you want to make casual conversation with me while waiting in line, please note: if the child in my trolley is wearing pink, she is a girl. Furthermore, if I have chips, ice-cream, and five extra-large jars of Nutella in my trolley, this does not give you licence to say, 'Oh, having a party, are you?' No, I am not. The treats are for me.

### Dear Groovy Young Person,
Yes, you may interact with my child and laugh at her antics. Yes, you may comment on how cute she is. But don't be surprised if I ask you to mind her for a minute or few as I run to the milk aisle or pop out to grab a cappuccino. You started the conversation, honey. She's all yours!

## Sick and Tired

# Inpatient Insights

*A*s a parent, there is nothing worse than to see your child unwell, and I am grateful every single day that I have three wonderfully healthy children. Happily for me, I have had only rare experiences with my children being seriously ill; although, like any parent, I've had my share of doctors' appointments and late-night runs to the emergency department.

When Pinkela was eighteen months she developed scarlet fever as a complication of chicken pox. The GP had warned me that her fever could remain high, and so determined was I not to worry that I stayed calm even as a red rash crept over her entire torso and down each limb. By the time I realised it was definitely appropriate to panic and rushed her into hospital, she was in toxic shock and required emergency treatment. Though quickly out of danger, she spent a gruelling ten days in isolation on intravenous antibiotics, which she withstood with heartbreaking fortitude. She barely winced as the needles were reinserted into her little arm, night after night after night. I think it would have been easier if she had cried.

More recently, Toddler stayed a night in hospital after a scary incident involving a friend's house, a cupboard, and a pill of unknown origin. It was a shocking experience for her, for me, and not least my poor guilt-stricken friend. Thankfully, Toddler made a full recovery. And my friend will be fine too one day, when the emotional scars have healed.

I learned some valuable lessons from my two visits to the children's hospital. The most important of these is that if you get to take your child home, then you are indeed one of the lucky ones. But there are other, slightly less profound lessons that enlightened me about human nature, and helped me to wipe the unpleasant fuzz off my teeth without the assistance of a toothbrush.

## What I Learned in Hospital

♀ *In the face of a medical crisis, a grandmother will attempt to feed her grandchild biscuits. This is true even – or especially – when the grandchild is on her way to the emergency room. It is an instinctive reaction over which the grandmother has no control, and it is utterly useless for the parent to attempt to resist.*

♀ *Private health insurance, status and connections are of no consequence when trying to secure a private hospital room for your child. The most effective way to get your own room is for your child to scream ferociously and continuously for four hours, disturbing every other child and carer in the six-bed ward. This is marvellous as the private rooms have a pull-out parent bed, which can be used to sleep in during the two (non-consecutive) hours of the night your child is no longer crying.*

♀ *When the nice nurses call you 'Mum' it is lovely. When the mean nurses call you 'Mum' it makes you want to slap them.*

♀ *In the absence of a toothbrush or toothpaste, baby wipes make an effective and fragrant tooth cleaner (although I would recommend rinsing with water afterwards to get rid of the floral taste).*

♀ *When the nurse tells you the doctor is 'on his way', he is, indeed, on his way.*

♀ *Being 'on his way' could mean he shows up anytime from five minutes to four and a half hours later. It is best not to wait up.*

♀ *Play therapists are wonderful people. They dress up as clowns, provide toys and books, and blow bubbles to distract the little patients during procedures, all of which are, indeed, beautiful ideas. Giving the bottle of bubbles to the patient after the procedure so that she can fling it all over herself and her hospital bed? Not quite so beautiful.*

♀ *When your child wrenches out the cannula from her arm, it is appropriate to stay calm, apply pressure, and call for the nurse. At least, so I hear. As my tendency is to become panicked, yell, 'Oh no! Oh no!' as blood spurts around the room, and run around in circles, I can't really say for sure.*

♀ *There is no excuse for hospital food. Really. None. Boiled lifeless vegetables, depressed slices of some unidentified animal, and French fries that resemble pale dead fingers slumped on the plate do nothing to inspire confidence, raise spirits, or promote recovery. It is far more uplifting to eat the chips from the vending machine. More nutritious, too.*

♀ *The nursing staff and doctors of our hospitals deserve our support, thanks and deep appreciation.*

# A Giant Pain

Nothing can prepare you for the worry you feel when your child is ill. Nothing can prepare you for how hot their foreheads can get. Nothing can prepare you for how frighteningly lethargic they become. And nothing – *nothing* – can prepare you for how much vomit actually comes out of their little bodies.

What's more, nothing teaches you to know exactly when something is wrong with your child. Children, as we know, don't come with an instruction manual, and as parents, we can't always tell when they are genuinely ill. We have all been guilty of yelling at our child for being lazy or having a tantrum, only to discover three hours later that they are sick and burning with fever. (At least, I hope you all have. I'd hate to think I'm the only one.) On the other hand, we've all been fooled by our kids, believing them when they miserably announce that they feel poorly and think that they will have to stay home, only to find them merrily playing Wii and munching on toast once the threat of being taken to school has passed.

Having a child who is truly ill is a source of terrible anguish. Having a child who is a bit sick ... well ... that's just a giant pain. Believe me; I've had plenty of experience.

## It Hurts

♀ Toddler had an infection but refused to take her medicine. After bribery and threats failed, I held her down and forced some medicine into her mouth, but she spat it out. Determined, I forced her down again, and got some more medicine into her mouth. She swallowed, glared at me, and projectile vomited the medicine all over the room. I gave up and hoped the infection would just pass.

♀ Toddler had a fever but refused to take her Panadol. Remembering the projectile vomiting incident, I bought her some rectal suppositories. As I tried to insert one into her, she kicked me and the suppository flew across the room. I gave up and hoped the fever would just pass.

♀ Little Man felt hot. Tired of having to hold a thermometer under a wiggly arm, I told him that he was a big boy now, and that it was time to put the thermometer under his tongue. Little Man put the thermometer firmly in his mouth, bit down hard, broke the thermometer in two, and swallowed the mercury. I spent a relaxing evening on the phone to Poisons Information. Turns out he didn't have a temperature after all.

♀ Toddler pulled up her T-shirt to show me quite a horrendous rash. 'Does it hurt?' I asked. 'Yes!' she told me plaintively. I touched the rash. It felt hot. I touched her forehead. It felt hot. I gave her a drink and called the doctor. When I returned, Toddler had spilt the drink on herself. I wiped it off. The rash wiped off with it.

♀ After Little Man developed a worryingly husky voice, I took him to the ear, nose and throat specialist, concerned about growths on his vocal cords. 'This can happen when a child yells a lot,' the doctor said. 'Does he have a loud voice?' 'Not particularly,' I answered. 'MUM! I WANT TO GO HOME!' Little Man screamed. The ENT specialist smiled and showed us to the door.

♀ *'Ooh, my back hurts,' said Toddler. I examined her carefully. She seemed okay. 'Ooh, my back hurts,' said Toddler, again. I gave her a back rub and propped her on pillows in front of her favourite TV show. 'Ooh, my back hurts,' she repeated for the third time. I dialled the doctor. As the phone rang, I heard the television. 'Ooh, my back hurts,' one of the characters was saying. I hung up the phone.*

♀ *The nurse called from Pinkela's school. Apparently Pinkela had been going to her office three to four times a week complaining of 'feeling funny'. The nurse suggested that she get a full medical check-up. 'Why do you keep going to the nurse?' I asked Pinkela that night. 'Because she's nice,' Pinkela answered. 'And I get to lie on her bed.' I didn't bother making the appointment.*

♀ *The director from Toddler's crèche called. 'She seems a bit poorly,' the director said, 'and she'll probably sleep better at home. I think you'd better pick her up.' I picked Toddler up. She was so excited to be home that she sang and danced the entire afternoon. The next time I got a call from the crèche, I let it go through to voicemail.*

♀ *Toddler was sick with a bacterial infection, and I was required to take wee samples. This entailed hovering near Toddler waiting for her to wee, then holding a container optimistically around her nether regions as she did so. It involved getting rather wet, and wasn't at all fun.*

♀ *Toddler was sick with a gut infection, and I was required to take poo samples. This was actually too horrible to write about.*

♀ *'I very sick, Mummy,' Toddler told me. 'Where?' I asked. 'Here,' she said, pointing to her tummy. 'Ouch. It hurters me.' I rushed to the doctor. 'I think she has appendicitis,' I told him. The doctor lay her down. 'Where does it hurt, dear?' he asked. 'Here!' said Toddler, resolutely. She was pointing to her toe.*

# Anyone Else Would Be in Hospital

There's no greater strain on a marriage than a case of Man Flu. The sick husband is an utter nightmare. Though the average man would cut off his own hand to escape death when trapped in a rock climbing fall (although this hasn't happened to The Architect, probably because he's never actually gone rock climbing), he will experience the flu as an agony which rightfully would require hospitalisation, were he not so incredibly brave. He will then recline on the couch, moaning, demanding 'fluids' and announcing that he feels 'weak', as his wife downs two paracetamol to cope with her own headache, and feeds and bathes the kids on her own.

When The Architect gets sick, he effectively becomes single again. He takes to his bed, relinquishing all responsibilities as husband and father. He asks pathetically for cold flannels and aspirin. He complains of his dangerously high fever, which upon measurement turns out to be a reasonably safe 37.3 degrees. He aches all over. He has a headache and nausea. And then he requests some soup and sits up cheerily in bed, eating a hearty dinner and watching *Top Gear*.

And God help you when a man notices any 'symptom' not attributable to hunger or fatigue. Recently, for example, The Architect developed a sudden and alarming case of 'tongue cancer', a shocking condition which to my untrained eye looked remarkably like a case of 'bit my tongue'. He spent two days agonisingly awaiting his doctor's appointment, all the while bidding me farewell and planning his own funeral. On the morning of the appointment, miraculously enough, the tongue cancer went into remission.

## Man Flu Symptoms: A Diagnostic Tool

- A vague sensation of 'weakness', particularly upon exertion (notably housework and childcare duties).
- Profound exhaustion, ruling out activities such as visits to the in-laws or grocery shopping. The exhaustion does not, however, preclude full participation in agreeable pursuits such as going to the cricket, hanging with friends, or joining one's family for pizza.
- A dry throat, temporarily eased by the administration of fluids. In healthy individuals, this is known as 'thirst'.
- Mild nausea, temporarily eased by the administration of food. In healthy individuals, this is known as 'hunger'.
- Mild depression, temporarily eased by the administration of a favourite TV show. In healthy individuals, this is known as 'boredom'.
- The urge to blow nose noisily and gustily at regular intervals, combined with the inability to direct used tissues into an appropriate receptacle, resulting in a litter of dirty tissues all over the bedroom floor.
- A female partner who has recently become unwell. The male immune system is compromised when his mate is ill, and he will inevitably become debilitated at the exact time she needs his assistance. Often his symptoms will exactly mirror hers, but with far greater severity. If she has a headache he will develop a

*migraine. If she has backache, he will be unable to walk. If she has a fever, he will fall into a coma. Happily, when his partner's condition improves the male recovers immediately.*

- *The urgent need for paracetamol or aspirin. The patient will only accept half the recommended adult dose in order to prove his manly strength, but will continue to complain about his desperate ill health.*

- *Extreme courage. Anyone else experiencing his level of agony would definitely be in hospital.*

# Men Collapse, Women Soldier On

To be fair, I get sick, too; it's just that I am not permitted to acknowledge it. This is because it is impossible to be ill when you're a mother. For a start, there simply isn't time; after all, it's hard enough to find a moment to go to the toilet uninterrupted, let alone rest in bed for a week or two. For another thing, your family will simply not accept it, a fact I experienced firsthand during my bout of glandular fever.

'Mum? GET OUT OF BED!' Little Man commanded, as I lay feeble and feverish under the duvet.

'I'm sick, sweetie,' I whispered pathetically.

'There's NOTHING WRONG WITH YOU,' he announced sternly. 'Now GET UP.'

Pinkela, who was then only a preschooler, joined in the protests. 'You're not sick, Mama!' she insisted, scrambling on the bed and bouncing perilously close to my pounding head. 'Wake up! Wake up! Wake up!'

The Architect, too, refused to believe that I was incapacitated. It was far too confronting. Not only did this mean that he would have to take care of me, it meant that he would have to take care of the kids. Alone. And who could be expected to do that?

'I'm really sick,' I told him one day, having been forced to return to bed after breakfast. The Architect seemed to find it hard to process this information.

'You'll be okay after a good night's sleep,' he said.

'I slept for eleven hours last night,' I whimpered.

'You've had a very busy day,' he told me.

'But it's only ten a.m.'

Now, in most circumstances, I would struggle on, cooking and cleaning and chauffeuring the kids with only Panadol to soothe my pounding head. However, not even a battle-hardened mother can cope with a beast like glandular fever, and after several failed attempts to climb out of bed and a temperature reading of 39.5 degrees, even The Architect was forced to acknowledge I was, indeed, ill.

And this, of course, was where Testosterone Man kicked in. The Architect told the kids I was sick and that they needed to behave ('Does that mean we can watch TV?' Little Man asked. 'As much as is humanly possible,' he replied) and took control. He cooked dinner (okay, he warmed up dinner, but effort, not quality, counts). He made the school lunches. He bathed the kids. He did everything I had no idea he could do because he'd never actually done it before. What's more, he did it all with that proud, puffed-up 'Look at me! I'm Superdad!' expression on his face, which made me *really* cross, because it's *bloody hard work* and he was *deliberately* making it look easy to *torment* me.

Or perhaps I was just being a little sensitive because I was sick.

Either way, I realised that my husband can cope, and that the world won't fall apart if I collapse. Unfortunately, though, I have to have a temperature of 39.5 to collapse, which is not something that happens very often. Still, I suppose I don't need to be strictly honest about how high my temperature is. After all, a mother's work is never done, and I need to do *something* to get some rest around here.

## Feeding Time

## Food Foibles

*W*hen I embarked on motherhood I knew that food would become a very important issue. The desire to feed is somehow stimulated post-natally in the soul of the new mother, complementing, in my case, the lifelong desire to eat.

So it didn't surprise me when the sight of my baby swallowing mashed banana gave me one of the greatest highs of my life (although admittedly, I had been a little sheltered). Sadly, the high didn't last long. Feeding my children, I discovered, can be complicated indeed.

Each of my three kids has a unique relationship to food, and one that provides significant challenges for me. For a start (considering he was the first), let's look at my son.

Little Man turned out to be a very poor eater. Actually, when I think about it, 'poor' isn't the right term to use. You can't be poor at something you don't actually do.

Every meal starts the same. Little Man sits at the table, asks 'how many bites' he has to eat, halves that number, halves it again then claps his hand over his mouth after the second bite. Whether it's frankfurters, noodles, cheese, or Vegemite on toast, he is full after two mouthfuls. I've tried being strict, being lenient, forcing him to sit, allowing him to roam, providing one choice only, offering a buffet-style selection – it makes not the slightest bit of difference. The child is not interested in food. It's lucky I saw him come out of my body or I would worry he is not my genetic offspring.

Pinkela, on the other hand, is very clearly my daughter. She has an excellent appetite. This would be wonderful, except that her appetite is actually so excellent she will happily eat everything that is not nailed down. She eats anything, and she eats at any time. She asks for tuna after breakfast. She asks for chips after lunch. She asks for cheese and crackers as I'm tucking her into bed. And mealtimes become a race to get to her brother's food. 'No, thank you, Mum,' he has barely finished saying, before she'll snatch the chop out of his hand, gleefully shouting, 'I'll have it!' The two of them are like Jack Spratt and his wife, except that my son eats neither lean nor fat, and my daughter eats lots of both.

As for Toddler, well, she is just infuriating. The child messes with my mind. One day she loves sausages. The next day she hates sausages. One week she loves noodles. The next week noodles are 'stupid'. One minute she'll want cheese. The next minute she's shredding her cheese into small pieces and scattering it on the carpet. The only thing she has ever consistently enjoyed over a period of time is chocolate, and even that is generally smeared all over her face and clothes as much as it is put into her mouth.

Happily, however, The Architect is easy to please. He will eat absolutely any meat, provided that it is crumbed and deep-fried in oil. He will eat absolutely any vegetable, provided that it is potato. And he will eat absolutely any salad, provided that it is small enough to fit on one fork.

As for me, well, I eat anything. I just prefer for it not to be cooked by myself.

# Fruit Does Not Count as Dessert

*A*s every person knows, parents are supposed to set the rules, and kids are supposed to adapt to them. However, as every *parent* knows, kids set their own rules about pretty much everything. The role of the parent is to figure out these rules and try to work with them as best as possible.

There is no area in which this is more true than food. Every child has their own idiosyncratic rules about food that no parent is able to change. Peas must be mashed into potato. Peas must not come in contact with potato. Apples must be peeled. Apples must be sliced. Apples must be cut into cubes and served on toothpicks. Meat must be hot. Meat must be cold. Meat must be diced and drenched in tomato sauce.

My kids are no exception. Toddler, for example, requires the inclusion of cheese with every meal, whether it's breakfast, lunch, dinner or a bedtime snack. Pinkela requires her meat to be arranged in slices in an attractive pattern on her plate, preferably a flower, or a heart, or a 'shape that looks like something real'. And Little Man insists upon every food group being separated and presented in a different bowl, so that he can taste it, nibble it, and reject it in turn without contaminating the other ingredients.

Their guidelines might be vexatious, their guidelines might even be illogical, but if I want them to eat, I have to comply.

But these are just my kids' particular food rules. There are also universal laws of food that apply to nearly every young person in the western world. Laws that are immutable, kind of like the laws of physics (which I assume are immutable; I never understood them all that well).

Laws we parents can struggle against, but will never defeat.

## *Food Rules*

- ♀ *Mealtimes provide merely a rough guideline. Hunger can strike at any moment.*
- ♀ *Whatever is in your friend's lunch box is much more desirable than your lunch.*
- ♀ *Whatever is at the school tuckshop is much more desirable than your lunch.*
- ♀ *When dining out, the more expensive the meal, the less of it you should eat.*
- ♀ *The purpose of chocolate is to be eaten immediately. This is true of chocolate in the fridge, chocolate in Nana's fridge, chocolate in Mum's friend's fridge, chocolate in the supermarket aisle, chocolate at the petrol station, and chocolate in the box being presented to someone as a gift.*
- ♀ *Chocolate milk does not count as actual chocolate.*
- ♀ *Nutella does not count as actual chocolate.*
- ♀ *It is unthinkable to go to bed without dessert.*
- ♀ *Fruit does not count as dessert.*
- ♀ *A long car journey requires snacks. 'Long' refers to anything over ten minutes.*
- ♀ *Food can be a great way to buy time, particularly when Mum wants to leave the house. Milk can take over half an hour to*

*sip with a straw, and an apple can take at least an hour when nibbled at a leisurely pace.*

♀ *Any discarded bits of chewed food should be passed directly to Mum, or stored in her handbag.*

♀ *Serviettes are for decorative purposes only. Fingers and mouths should be wiped on clothing.*

♀ *Lollies do not count as food because they are small.*

♀ *If food is green, it is bad, unless it is a lolly.*

♀ *If food is 'healthy', it is bad.*

♀ *If food has seeds in it, it is bad.*

♀ *If food has 'bits' in it, it is bad.*

♀ *If food is individually wrapped it will taste better.*

♀ *If food is in a packet with compartments, it will taste better.*

♀ *If food comes in a packet with a picture of a Pokemon, Teletubby or Fairy on it, it will taste better.*

♀ *If food comes with a toy, it will taste better.*

♀ *If food has a shape that resembles nothing found in nature, it will taste better.*

♀ *If food has a colour that resembles nothing found in nature, it will taste better.*

♀ *If food has a name resembling nothing found in nature, it will taste better.*

♀ *If food is served on plates going round on a train, it will taste better.*

♀ *If food can be thrown, it will be.*

♀ *If food can be used as body butter, it will be.*

♀ *It food can be used as wall paint, it will be.*

♀ *Eating sugar directly from the bowl is the ultimate high.*

# Forget MASTERCHEF

*T*here are people who love cooking, and they fascinate me. I would quite like to be married to one of them. As someone who loves *eating*, I think the relationship would work quite well. The Architect claims to love cooking, but he doesn't really. What he actually loves to do is watch cooking shows, particularly when Nigella Lawson is hosting, which to me does not appear to be the same thing. After all, an hour spent salivating in front of the television generally doesn't produce anything tangible in the way of a meal.

Cooking for me is a chore, not a hobby. It is something that needs to be done every night (using 'every' in the sense of 'most') so that my family will have dinner on the table – or at least on their laps in front of the TV. It is not 'fun', it is not a 'passion', and I am about as likely to appear as a contestant on *MasterChef* as I am on *Strictly Come Dancing*.

And if you've seen me on the dance floor lately, you'll understand just how strong a statement that is.

## Why I Hate Cooking

♀ Cooking invariably involves a great deal of mess, which requires a great deal of cleaning. The reason I cook is to eat, not to clean.

♀ Certainly there is intrinsic satisfaction in preparing a meal then watching your loved ones enjoy it. But considering the preparation takes approximately two hours, and the eating takes approximately seven minutes, there is proportionally greater satisfaction in ironing a shirt.

♀ There has never been an occasion when everyone in my family has wanted the same thing to eat at the same time. And that includes the early days of my marriage when there was only The Architect and me.

♀ I struggle to choose between Vegemite on toast and peanut butter on toast in the mornings. Choosing an evening meal creates small explosions in my brain.

♀ When a meal idea does come to me, I want it now. I do not want to wait for two hours while it cooks.

♀ Preparing food requires tasting, and tasting food makes me want to eat it. So I end up eating the equivalent of two or three meals before the food has even made it to the table.

♀ I am constantly burning myself on the stove. Not only does this cause pain and scarring, but I must explain to Toddler that Mummy is screaming in delight because her food is so delicious. Having tasted my food, she knows this is not the case.

♀ Any recipes with exotic or foreign-sounding ingredients scare me. And recipes without exotic or foreign-sounding ingredients tend to be called 'chops'.

♀ Following a recipe is boring. Diverting from a recipe leads to monstrous offerings such as jam chicken and liquid beef.

♀ It seems such a waste to go to all that effort when takeaway is just one phone call away.

♀ *No matter what I make, the children prefer frankfurters.*

♀ *No matter what I make, The Architect prefers schnitzel.*

♀ *No matter what I make, I prefer Nutella.*

♀ *No matter what I make, I'm really just killing time before dessert.*

# Creative Cooking

*T*he biggest problem with cooking is that I have to do it. Though I feel comfortable refusing many of my family's requests – to play Twister, to wear silly hats to the shops, to buy a boat, to pole dance (okay, so pole dancing is just The Architect's request) – I cannot refuse their demands for food. And unfortunately, human beings need feeding every day. Several times. We are very inefficient that way.

As a result, I am very creative with my meal preparation (using 'creative' in the sense of 'lazy'). Breakfasts and lunches aren't generally an issue – even I can manage cereal and sandwiches – but when it comes to dinners, my meals can fail to dazzle.

Now, I'm not always a culinary disgrace. I do sometimes whip up a roast beef with three veg, and it is good. However, this is generally only when guests are coming over and I wish to impress them. Quite frankly, such a feast would be wasted on my family. Little Man won't eat it, The Architect will complain that it's not fried, and Toddler will fling her portion on the floor. Pinkela, of course, will happily scoff it down, but then Pinkela would happily scoff down a margarine sandwich, so that doesn't really count for much.

So, more often than not, I take short cuts. I offer the bare minimum that my family will accept (and, frequently, somewhat less than that). I make meals that would make Nigella Lawson weep. I make meals that often make my son weep. Still, they may not be gourmet, they may not be particularly nutritious, they may not even be tasty, but at least they are filling. And they will carry us all over till breakfast, which is all I'm really aiming for.

For at breakfast, as I said, even I can manage cereal.

## You Call This Dinner?

- ♀ Noodles with melted cheese.
- ♀ Noodles without melted cheese.
- ♀ McDonald's.
- ♀ Takeaway pizza.
- ♀ Takeaway chicken and chips.
- ♀ Takeaway chips. (There's no point getting the chicken as they're not going to eat it anyway.)
- ♀ Anything bought warm from a shop.
- ♀ Baked beans.
- ♀ Tinned tuna.
- ♀ Boiled eggs.
- ♀ Reheated leftover from last night's dinner.
- ♀ Reheated leftovers from my mother's house.
- ♀ Reheated leftovers from a restaurant meal.
- ♀ Reheated leftovers that have been frozen for about six months.
- ♀ Leftovers from lunch, but this time presented on a platter.
- ♀ Anything microwaved on high for three minutes.
- ♀ Anything that comes before dessert.
- ♀ Anything put on a plate in the evening.

## Motherhood Mindless Eating

*M*y eating habits have changed dramatically since I became a mother. These days, I don't always have time to prepare my own food, so busy am I preparing food for my kids (or, until recently, *producing* food from my very own chest). And there is always so much else to do. Laundry, homework, shopping, bathing, tidying, cleaning, vacuuming, sweeping... Satisfying my hunger remains a very high priority, but creating a gourmet meal for this hunger comes lower than, say, having a shower or doing a wee. So while the quantity of food remains the same, the quality has diminished significantly since giving birth.

Then there is the problem of exhaustion. A gourmet meal is nice, but it's hard to savour a braised duck with caramelised shallots when you keep losing consciousness in the middle of a meal. If there's a choice between a slice of toast followed by a sleep or a gastronomic feast that will keep me at the stove and table for two hours, I can assure you that I will always choose toast.

Most significantly, though, there is the issue of proximity. I used to handle food only at mealtimes, with the exception of the takeaway cappuccinos that would punctuate my day. I now spend half my life handling food – buying it, preparing

196

it, cooking it, feeding it to my kids, retrieving it from their mouths, or simply watching it as it is being eaten. Food is there, all the time. And because my hands are so very close to my mouth, it is inevitable that a fair amount of the stuff will make its way into my stomach. Often, without me even realising.

## Yum, Yum

- ♀ *I lick Toddler's repulsive ice lolly because it's dripping all over my hand and I don't have any wipes.*
- ♀ *I eat jelly beans straight out of Little Man's mouth because he wants to spit them out and I can't find a bin.*
- ♀ *I eat a plastic cheese stick that's been in my bag for a month because I'm peckish and it's the closest food on hand.*
- ♀ *I don't bother making myself breakfast, eating instead the crusts from my children's toast.*
- ♀ *I eat plates and plates of leftover hot chips because ... well ... they're there.*
- ♀ *I absentmindedly polish off a revolting, partially masticated rice bubble bar I'm supposed to be minding for Pinkela, which makes her cry when she returns for her snack.*
- ♀ *I spend hours creating a gourmet dinner for myself and The Architect, only to polish off the kids' leftover noodles and frankfurters at six p.m.*
- ♀ *I give up making gourmet dinners for myself and The Architect, and make noodles and frankfurters for the entire family.*
- ♀ *I buy 'treat' foods for the kids, and end up eating them all when the kids are asleep.*
- ♀ *I buy 'treat' foods for the kids that I know they don't even like.*

# Part Three: Me

## Besties and Best-Nots

## My Glue

*F*riendships are the glue that holds us individuals together. Without my friends, I would have come unstuck about a week into the parenting journey. I simply cannot imagine my life as a mother without them.

I was lucky enough to stumble upon a wonderful group of women when my son was about seven weeks old. We were six new mums, vaguely known to each other, who agreed – some more enthusiastically than others – to form a mothers' group. As we were all first-timers, none of us had the slightest idea about how to deal with these tiny noisy people who had turned our lives upside down. Ultimately, of course, it was this shared naivety that quickly endeared us to each other; after all, the last thing you need when you're struggling with a newborn is to be given unsolicited advice.

Initially, I was sceptical about joining a mothers' group. The girls seemed nice enough, but I wasn't sure I had anything more in common with any of them than the fact that we'd each grown a baby in our wombs. How wrong I was. Over the past eleven years, I have grown to love and depend on my mothers' group friends like sisters, and we have shared every conceivable triumph and tragedy. Our initial group of six babies has grown to a troop of seventeen. There have been celebrations, deaths in our families, births and birthdays, miscarriages and illnesses, evictions and new houses, new jobs and a divorce. These women, their children and their partners mean everything to me, and I'm pretty sure I mean a lot to them, too.

Female friendships are based on sharing. We talk, endlessly. We celebrate each other's successes – because for women, an achievement means nothing if there is no one with whom to share it. We console and comfort each other through our challenges and difficulties.

Friendships don't change after we have children; all that changes is the nature of the experiences we share. Before children we talk about work and men and parents and friends and our bodies and the world around us. And when we become mothers we talk about all things babies – of nights of broken sleep, of sore nipples and leaking nappies, of meltdowns and milestones, of tantrums and temperatures, and toddlers and teething and traumas. Of course, we still occasionally talk about work and men and parents and friends and our bodies and the world around us. But we talk about babies a *lot*.

Not only am I lucky enough to have my mothers' group in my life, I also have a handful of other precious friends who form the backbone of my world. The extent to which women nurture each other cannot be overstated. Whether it's advice, reassurance, assistance, or gifts of chocolate and alcohol when all else fails, good friends can be the greatest support a woman can have.

Toxic friends, on the other hand, are another story altogether...

# Toxic Friends

*M*otherhood is the great equaliser, where all can be equally skilled, or, more likely, hopelessly incompetent. Your age, your intellect, your professional standing, your qualifications, your wealth ... none of it matters whatsoever to the tiny infant howling in your arms.

Motherhood can, though, bring out traits in women that were not previously apparent, or wildly exaggerate traits that had already been evident. Competitiveness. Neuroses. Smugness. Envy. Traits which can drain you of your energy and sap you of your self-esteem. Traits which can tear old friends apart, and cause new acquaintances to reel back in horror. Traits which make for a toxic friend.

It can be difficult to identify a toxic friend, until a certain number of interactions have transpired. Initially they may seem ideal. They are highly curious, extremely concerned with your business, and skilled at eliciting information. They also regale you with stories about their own life, which are wonderfully upbeat and positive. It's not until you walk away from the conversation feeling like the World's Worst Mother that you realise that, instead of being supportive and nurturing, this woman is actually just boasting about her own life and revelling in your misfortune, and by then, it is generally too late.

I've fallen victim to a number of toxic friends. I always like to hear myself talk, so I'm easy prey for anyone who wishes to dig for dirt. I'll open up immediately about the difficulties in my life, the stresses in my marriage, and the challenges of my kids. But then I'll hear the note of judgement in the other person's voice, or their slight hint of triumph as they compare themselves to me, and I realise I need to step back and protect myself, or I'll leave feeling very, very small.

## Things Toxic Friends Say

- My kids eat only organic food. They have never, ever tasted preservatives.
- The triplets have been sleeping through the night since I brought them home from the hospital. I think my calmness rubs off on them.
- Ooh, you do look tired, don't you?
- No, my kids don't watch any television, or play any electronic games. We read and play charades together at night. You should try it. It's very fulfilling.
- Thank you, yes, I do like taking care of my appearance. I could recommend some products that would work wonders on you.
- Oh, do you bottle-feed? No, I breastfed all my kids until they were three. It's far better for them, you know.
- Oh, do you let the baby sleep in your bed? Well, it's certainly not what I would do. But each to her own.
- Not that I mean to brag, but my daughter just received her eighteenth Merit Certificate for the year. How's your little girl doing? Still struggling?

🔌 *I'm finishing up my doctorate this year. I have so much spare time now that I'm home with a baby. What are you doing to keep busy?*

🔌 *Oh, my husband is an absolute angel. I couldn't ask for more.*

🔌 *No, I don't have any household help. I find the housework a breeze. It's just a question of being organised.*

🔌 *Send the kids to holiday camps? Oh no, I wouldn't dream of it! I like spending time with them in the break.*

🔌 *Does it bother your child that he is an only child/middle child/youngest of four/a mistake?*

🔌 *Does it bother your child that you work such long hours?*

🔌 *Is it true your son got suspended the other day? I'm so sorry to hear it.*

🔌 *We can't decide whether to let our son do soccer or cricket on Saturday mornings. He's so outstandingly good at both.*

🔌 *Oh! Your children are boisterous, aren't they? I'm not used to it. My girls are so quiet and serene.*

🔌 *How many after-school activities do your kids do? Oh, really? Is that all?*

🔌 *Yes, we love just popping the kids in the car and taking off on holidays. We're very spontaneous.*

🔌 *Sorry to hear things are so difficult for you. Everything is marvellous with me.*

🔌 *Oh no, I never eat sugar. It's poison, you know. But you go ahead.*

🔌 *Oh no, I never eat meat. It's murder, you know. But you go ahead.*

🔌 *Oh no, I never drink alcohol. I don't need it to have a good time. But you go ahead.*

🔌 *No, this four-course meal with matching wines was no trouble! I cook like this most nights anyway.*

🔌 *We make love four or five nights a week. I adore it. How often do you?*

↳ *We're just so lucky with our son. So gifted and handsome and a wonderful sportsman, too.*

↳ *We bought a house on the French Riviera because we were tired of the old beach house. It's so important to give the kids experience of different cultures, don't you think?*

# Really Must Get Together Soon

*M*any new friends have come into my life since I've become a parent. Aside from my beautiful mothers' group, I've met other wonderful women (and men) through preschool and school. And while I've forged lifelong bonds with some, I've met many who are perfectly nice, but with whom I just don't feel that magical zing – that spark of connection that makes me actually want to meet them for a coffee. Or, to be honest, talk to them for more than two minutes.

Now, not having a connection with someone is no problem at all when the feeling is mutual, but it can be rather challenging when the other person is trying to befriend me. You see, I have discovered that – just as I don't automatically like the children of my friends – I also don't automatically like the parents of my kids' friends. Take the mother who always sends her child for play dates, but who has never, ever reciprocated the favour. Or the father who is loud and obnoxious, always lingering too long when he picks up his child. And the mother who knows everything about everything, and will not be satisfied until she has identified at least one ailment in my household and proffered a solution, either herbal or psychological. Or the many, many others who are perfectly lovely people, but just don't ring my bells in any special way.

So why can't I just be nice and meet them for a coffee anyway? Well, since having kids, I regard free time as a rare and precious commodity that should only be spent on those I really like. If I've got my children with me, I'd rather be in the company of people who make me feel good about myself as a person and a mother. And any free time without kids is so rare and precious that I wish to spend it only with people I truly love.

So how do I gently prevent acquaintances from morphing into superfluous friends? And how do I let down the friends I no longer wish to spend time with? Harsh as it may sound, there have been times when I've needed to end a friendship that is already in existence. Perhaps our different styles of parenting have made us incompatible. Perhaps my friend is competitive, and makes me feel inadequate about my mothering, my messy home, and my fridge full of preservatives. Or perhaps I don't approve of her parenting skills, especially the way she forces her kids to recite Shakespeare at breakfast and attend Little Genius workshops every afternoon. Or perhaps we've just grown apart.

It's difficult terminating a friendship, and it is not at all like terminating a romantic relationship. Romances must be ended definitely. You must announce that they're over and provide reasons why (for example, 'I'm moving overseas', 'It's not you, it's me', 'I've found someone else' or 'You're boring and ugly'), and the words 'break up' must be employed. Friendships are different. Friendships develop gradually and – according to the unspoken rules of relationships – must be allowed to end gradually, too.

We all know the protocol. If you don't like someone anymore, you just contact them less and less. You make excuses, you don't return their calls for several days, and you make arrangements as infrequently as possible. Before you know it, your relationship has been downgraded. After a decent period of time you stop calling altogether, and then, by tacit agreement, the friendship is over. No awkward confrontation, no tears, no messy break-up.

Now, I would have downgraded a friend or two in my time, it's just that they all downgraded me first. Claire, for example. We met a few years back when our kids started preschool together. We seemed headed for a friendship but then things just didn't work out. We had nothing in common, our kids didn't get along, and she was horrified when I spilt a cup of coffee on her brand-new cream rug.

One day I called Claire and she never called back. I suspected I'd been downgraded, but needed confirmation. A week later I saw her at preschool and asked if she got my message. 'Yes, I did,' she said with a serene smile. That was all the confirmation I needed.

Still, as painful as being downgraded can be, you can also use the process to your advantage. If your unwanted friend isn't responding to your attempts to keep them at bay, then you can turn the tables. Make yourself as unappealing as possible and before you know it, she'll be coughing nervously in the school playground, backing away while muttering something about how you 'really must get together soon'.

## *What To Say To Get Yourself Downgraded*

🥿 *Can you believe all three of my kids have lice again? They seem to have it all the time these days! I have it too, actually. Look! You can see them crawling in my hair!*

🥿 *Be careful around me, I have a wicked case of herpes. It's highly infectious, you know.*

🔺 No, I've completely stopped using soap or deodorant. They disturb the natural oils in the skin.

🔺 Have I told you about that sex dream I had about your husband? It was hot.

🔺 Have I told you about that lesbian dream I had about you? It was hot.

🔺 We're thinking of joining a swingers' group – want to join us?

🔺 I'd love to meet for coffee sometime. I can tell you all about my favourite elements on the periodic table.

🔺 I'm so tired today. I was up late again last night playing the fruit machines while the kids slept in the car.

🔺 I was so desperate for some chocolate last night that I ate the cake I threw in the bin two days ago.

🔺 Please feel free to drop over, although you'll need to take off your shoes and remove any jewellery that might scratch the furniture.

🔺 Please feel free to drop over, as long as you don't mind getting naked. We have a nude home.

🔺 Please feel free to drop over. Just use the antibacterial wash at the door before you come in. Can't be too careful, you know.

🔺 You must come with me to my next spiritual meeting. We speak in tongues.

🔺 I'd love to come to dinner. I only eat white foods and drink clear liquids. That's not too much trouble, is it?

🔺 Please don't be alarmed if I yell obscenities or lash out at you. I came off my medication recently.

🔺 You have such a vivid green aura. I would love to lay my hands on you.

# *Leave a Message*

*I* love my mobile phone. Desperately. On the odd occasions I've left home without it – always accidentally, always with horror and regret – I've felt agitated and desperate, like I've gone out without my head. My phone is my link to the world, my security, my comfort. It tells me that I'll never be alone, that I can phone a friend anytime. It tells me that if I ever get caught in a locked toilet stall in a remote part of Westfield, I'll be able to call for help. (Not that this particular scenario has occurred yet, but it's good to be prepared.)

My phone is my version of my daughter's security blanket, only I don't put it in my mouth. Or sniff it. Or throw it on the floor and demand that other people pick it up. I do, however, cry when it gets lost.

Funnily enough, though, despite wanting to have my phone with me at all times, I don't actually like to answer it. And nine times out of ten, when I call one of my girlfriends on their mobile phones, they don't answer theirs, either. The fact is, we mothers text, we mothers voicemail, but we very rarely answer our phones.

For very good reason.

## Why I Don't Answer My Phone

🥿 If I'm out with my children, there is no point answering my phone, as my kids won't let me speak. They will inevitably choose the exact moment I say, 'Hello,' to loudly inform me of vital and urgent pieces of information that have until now remained unsaid (for example, that their school shoes are too small, that they don't like turnips, or that when they scratch their bottom, it tickles). It's far easier for me to let the call go through to voicemail, and to listen later, when I have time. Which, of course, is never. But still.

🥿 If I'm out without my kids, it means that they are at school or with a carer, and I have a maximum of a few hours to get anything done. On an average day, I may need to go to the butcher, go to the bank, buy Toddler some new pyjamas, get Pinkela her special organic eczema cream, go to the doctor's, renew my driver's licence and get my (annual) haircut, all within about an hour and a half. Time is of the essence. I do not wish to waste it on chatter. Again, voicemail is the answer.

🥿 Chances are I am at the supermarket. Now, despite the fact that I do a massive grocery shop at least once a week, I also have to stop and do 'top-up' shops approximately ... well ... every day. And for some reason, this does not excite me. So I generally do it at a rather brisk pace, running around the aisles like a crazed woman, grabbing things off shelves and flinging them into my trolley. I cannot afford to stop and chat on my phone, and I am not coordinated enough to chat and fling at the same time. So call me later.

🥿 If I am out and unencumbered, I know that any phone call is likely to be from my kids' carers. And I know that if one of my kids' carers call, they are unlikely to be sharing some delightful piece of happy news. The strongest possibility is that my child is a) unwell, b) infested with lice, or c) suspended. I don't like *doctors, I don't like lice, I don't like being called to the principal's office, and I certainly don't like picking up my kids in the middle of the day. In fact, if I'm out without my kids, I generally do not wish to be reminded that I have kids at all. Call me later. After I have picked up the kids. In which case you probably won't need to call me anyway.*

🔌 *A call on the mobile could very well be from The Architect. Generally when The Architect calls in the middle of the day it is either to talk about finances or to announce that he will be late home that night. Frankly, no good can come of either of those discussions. It is far preferable to ignore the call and hope that the financial problems will go away, and that he will arrive home early with a bunch of flowers, ready to cook dinner and bathe the kids.*

🔌 *A call on the mobile could be from my mother. Now, I love my mother dearly, but to stop and chat with her while I am rushing around is an inefficient use of my time. It is better to add value to the call by talking to my mum from home, while simultaneously cooking a chicken, brushing Pinkela's hair and helping Little Man with his homework. Also, this way I can hand the phone over to Toddler, who will babble meaninglessly to Nana for ten minutes or so. It may be incomprehensible, it may even make the phone sticky, but at least it will keep one child busy for a while.*

🔌 *A call on the mobile could be from another mum from my children's school, and then I would have to pretend to be interested in her. Even worse, I would have to pretend to be interested in her child. Much better to let the call go through to voicemail, and return it sometime in the rather distant, unspecified future.*

🔌 *A call on the mobile could be bad news. It's never a good idea to hear bad news far from home, away from the comforts of chocolate and alcohol. Better to wait.*

🥿 *A call on the mobile could be good news. Not a problem. The news will still be good later.*

🥿 *A call on the mobile is not going to be from Simon Baker. He doesn't have my number. So what's the point of answering?*

# You Have Mail

*N*ot only is it impossible to conduct a telephone conversation when you're a mum, it is also impossible to conduct a meaningful, face-to-face interaction with another adult while in the presence of your children. If you have ever attempted to talk to a girlfriend while a toddler is climbing all over you, gleefully tipping her babycino into your lap, and merrily rubbing Vegemite and toast into your hair, then you will know what I mean.

Which is why I am eternally grateful for the internet. The World Wide Web has changed the face of civilisation. It has revolutionised information exchange, business, research, global communication, war, politics, education, medicine, and every other aspect of our society. Most importantly, however, what it has really done is change the way I interact with my friends, family and colleagues.

As a mother, I greatly prefer the written to the spoken word. Given that I am never left alone to make a phone call, and outings with kids turn into adventures in child-wrangling, email is the only way I can effectively communicate with others. In fact, I would be quite happy never to use the phone again.

## Why I Love Email

- ♀ Every time I pick up the phone, three children drape themselves across me and start yelling – even if they've been sitting quietly on the other side of the room for the better part of the day. Of course, they still drape themselves across me and start yelling when I start typing, but at least I can keep typing with one hand and press send.

- ♀ I can email the same information to ten of my friends at once. Given that I no longer have time to call one of my friends, let alone ten, this is highly advantageous.

- ♀ I can fall asleep reading someone's email and they will never know. In conversations, closed eyes and drooling are a dead giveaway.

- ♀ It is difficult for me to finish a train of thought as I am interrupted by a child at least once per minute. With email I can write a cohesive paragraph, even if it does take the better part of a day.

- ♀ Due to my husband's selective deafness, he often misses important pieces of information that I tell him. If I send him emails using catchy titles such as 'Pictures of that porn star you think is hot' or 'I'm thinking of buying you this new sports car', I can be sure he's going to read them.

- ♀ Employers reading my emails can't see that I'm juggling a baby on my lap, supervising my kids' homework, and folding laundry while I'm working.

- ♀ Employers reading my emails can't see that I haven't changed my clothes for a week.

- ♀ Employers reading my emails can't see that I am smeared head to toe in Nutella.

- ♀ Employers reading my emails can't hear the baby screaming.

- ♀ Employers reading my emails can't hear me screaming.

## Looking *Good* Pretty Ordinary, Really

# Au Naturel? Au No!

*M*orning after morning my husband asks me how long a shower can possibly take.

And morning after morning, I give him the same answer: a long time.

Now, I don't want to have to stay in the bathroom for hours. I have plenty of other things I'd rather be doing. Like sleeping in. Or ... well, no, just sleeping in. But what we women have to do to become presentable in the morning is all consuming. Sometimes I feel like I've done a full day's work before I've even left the bathroom. And the older I get, the more work I have to do.

First I have to shampoo, detangle and condition, wash and deodorise, tweeze and shave (my legs, not my face, at least not yet). I have to cleanse, exfoliate and moisturise, slathering on whatever Cream of False Hope I am using at the moment. I have to brush and floss. And that's just to get to a point where I can fix my hair, bung on some eyeliner and whack on a bit of lippy.

Now, this morning routine is not fun. There is no pleasure in scraping a razor blade over my armpits, or plucking hairs from my nether regions, or scrubbing my face with cleansing microbeads (although I do like a nice nose pore strip, but that's more of a fetish, really). All of these chores take up so much time I barely have any moments left over to work, eat, or look after the kids.

No, my routine comprises the grooming essentials, the fundamentals of body maintenance required to make myself socially acceptable. And I haven't even touched on haircuts, fake tanning, body waxing or manicures.

Still, I *am* acting out of free will. At any stage, I could choose to reject society's norms, and embrace my body in its natural state. And who knows? Perhaps I would find deep fulfilment in being a hairy, pimpled, wrinkled, smelly woman with a monobrow and yellow teeth. Certainly I'd have a lot more time to engage in my favourite (though presumably solitary) pursuits.

From a feminist point of view, however, the whole grooming thing is unfair. The Architect doesn't need to spend any time in the bathroom other than showering, brushing his teeth, shaving, and having quality time on the loo. In fact, he doesn't even need to shave every day. An unshaven man can look rugged and sexy, with just a hint of 'bad boy' about him. I've even been known to request that The Architect doesn't shave for a couple of days to get that lovely 'Me Big Strong Testosterone Man' look (or at least as big and strong as my very short and slender husband will get).

But funnily enough my hubby has never requested the same of me. I've never heard him whisper seductively that he loves that sexy stubble when I haven't done my armpits in a while, or ask me to stop exfoliating for a week so he can get to that fabulous dead skin layer.

So for now, I'm keeping up my basic routine. But as for the haircut, fake tan, wax and manicure ... well, I'll get to them when I have time.

At this rate, when the kids graduate from high school. Or soon thereafter.

# When Good Faces Go Bad

Quick question: do you ever wake up, get dressed and made up, then look in the mirror and realise your face is on backwards? Because that happens to me. A lot.

They are called Bad Face Days. I go to bed looking perfectly normal. Attractive, even (you know ... for a forty-something mother of three). Then I fall asleep, and something mysterious happens overnight, because when I wake up in the morning, nothing is in the right place. There are strange creases on my cheeks. Bags under my eyes. Blotches everywhere. Puffiness where it should be hollow and hollowness where it should be puffy. Just ... *wrong*.

As for my hair, well, even though just yesterday it was all soft ringlets, today it looks as if a couple of steel wool pads have been partying hard on my head, dancing and trashing the joint, making love and having dozens of steel wool babies. Not good.

Of course, I can't go out looking like this, so I go into damage control. I get out my expensive mineral powder make-up (which I normally save for special occasions, as opposed to 'emergency intervention') and gently buff it on, as per the instructions. This doesn't seem to help, so I buff it on a little more firmly. This too seems ineffective, so I whack it on with the determination and aggression of a painter on the last section of a two-mile fence. As a result, I still look baggy and puffy and hollow, but with a thick layer of powder on my face. Fabulous.

So now I need lipstick, as my lips seem to have disappeared under all that powder, and eyeliner, to balance the scary brightness of my lips. And as I don't have time to wash my hair, I bundle it into a ponytail, giving me the overall appearance of a twelve-year-old girl going on stage to play the Wicked Witch. Nice.

There's no time to fix any of this mess, as the kids are late to school and it's better for them to be driven by someone who looks very much like a witch than for them to stay home with her all day. I take the kids to school, return straight home, and busy myself all morning, determined not to look in the mirror once until late in the afternoon. I hope that, somehow, under all the powder, my features will just magically realign themselves before pick-up time.

And if not, more drastic measures may need to be taken. Veil, anyone?

## Bad Face Day

- *My face looks too thin. This is interesting and somewhat perplexing, as my stomach looks too fat.*
- *The bags under my eyes have increased in size, from change purses, to clutches, to giant totes.*
- *Several of my eyebrow hairs are sticking out at right angles to my head, despite repeated applications of brow gel. Unwilling to pluck myself into bald oblivion, I spend the day looking like the unruly love child of Albert Einstein and an electrical socket.*

❥ *I have creases on my cheeks from sleeping on my side. Though they look endearingly 'cute' and 'rumpled' when I wake at six-thirty, the effect is 'old' and 'wrinkled' when they are still there after lunch.*

❥ *I have a pimple on my nose. This is completely unreasonable, as I am closer to menopause than adolescence, and it is simply not fair for anyone to have pimples and wrinkles at the same time.*

❥ *I have hairs growing where they really shouldn't – one out of my left nostril, one on my upper lip, and one, rather alarmingly, in the middle of my forehead. Of course, I only discover these when I'm in the car without tweezers, and spend the next two hours frantically and unsuccessfully trying to remove them with my fingernails.*

❥ *My complexion is less peaches and cream than strawberries and prunes. If you know what I mean.*

# It Really Catches the Light

Getting older isn't easy. I wouldn't describe myself as particularly vain, but I still find ageing confronting. My face is changing, and it's not for the better, and it's only going to be downhill from here on.

I wouldn't want to return to any earlier time in my life, but I certainly would like to have my younger face back. It was smooth and even and unlined and unmarked, and it radiated health and youth (and yes, I know that sounds a little like a skincare commercial, but it's true). Ironically, of course, I didn't appreciate my beautiful younger face because I was so obsessed with the tiny, tiny pimples I got every now and then. Now, as a wrinkled forty-one-year-old, I marvel at how gorgeous I was at eighteen. And no doubt when I'm sixty, I'll marvel at how gorgeous I was at forty-one, and feel sad that all I noticed were my tiny, tiny wrinkles.

Still, it's inevitable that we women get fixated on our flaws. (And it is, for the most part, women who agonise over their own imperfections. After all, you don't see many men obsessing about their wonky eyebrow hairs, or fretting that their left ear sticks out a couple of centimetres more than their right.)

Every woman hates at least one aspect of her appearance – her sparse eyelashes, her freckles, her big thighs, her big breasts, her small breasts, her thin hair, her straight hair, her impossibly curly hair – and often she will identify these horrendously disturbing traits all on her own. Frequently, too, a chance remark by a friend or acquaintance will lead to a lifelong obsession with one part of her anatomy. One of my friends is ridiculously self-conscious about some 'blotchiness' on her skin, which I have never been able to discern, but which was once pointed out to her by a beautician. Another hates her perfectly lovely bum, after a remark by her husband around twenty years ago.

As for me, it is my nose.

It started with a broken capillary, directly under my right nostril. Though no one had ever commented on it, it looked to me as if someone had drawn in red pen from my nose to my upper lip. I hated it and felt the world was staring at it in disbelief and repulsed horror. Finally, I made an appointment with the dermatologist to have the thing removed.

'I want this vein zapped,' I told him firmly. 'It's ruining my face.'

'What vein?' he asked. 'I can't see any vein.'

'This one,' I said impatiently, pointing it out. 'I'm very self-conscious about it.'

He peered closely at me and shrugged his shoulders.

'I'll do it if you want, but it's barely noticeable,' he told me.

'It's noticeable to me,' I said. 'Zap away.'

He took out his laser and began to work. 'Honestly, you can hardly see it,' he said. He finished lasering and stepped back. I looked in the mirror. The vein was gone.

'Brilliant!' I said. I felt elated, free of the hideous blemish that had been holding me back for so long. 'Thank you!'

'No problem,' he said. 'But really, I wouldn't have worried about it. What I would be concerned with is that old chicken pox scar.'

'What scar?' I asked him. 'I've never seen a scar.'

'This one,' he said, indicating with his gloved finger. 'It really catches the light.'

'Really?' I asked. I'd never noticed any scar. I peered more closely in the mirror. The doctor was right! There it was, a monstrosity of a thing, looming huge and cavernous on the bridge of my nose.

'Oh my God!' I exclaimed. 'It's terrible! Fix it! What can you do?'

'Nothing,' he said casually, peeling off his gloves. 'You'll just have to live with it.'

'But I can't!' I told him. 'It's awful! It's ruining my face!'

'Sorry,' he said and exited the room.

Since that dark moment, I have been obsessed with my scar. I stare at it in the mirror. I fantasise about how great my face would look without it. I comb the internet looking for miracle scar creams. And I spend hours trying to cover it with make-up.

But to this day, no one – not my husband, not my mother, not my friends, not any of my children – has ever even noticed it.

# Effort, Not Quality

*O*ur standards of appearance often drop after we have kids, even temporarily (which in my case means eleven years and counting). Prior to motherhood, I would not have considered leaving the house without a full face of make-up and a carefully coordinated outfit. Okay, so this is not strictly true; I used to wear lipstick and a T-shirt that matched my jeans, but I was always clean and tidy. For a long time after giving birth, however, I was proud of myself just for managing to leave the house. If I got changed out of my tracksuit pants before leaving the house, that was a wonderful bonus.

As for cleanliness, well, before kids I wouldn't have dreamed of going three days without washing my hair, whereas now I seriously consider whether I can go that third day without having a shower. Getting dressed may be a bonus, but having a shower before getting dressed is a bigger bonus still.

Still, as I always say, reducing standards isn't the same as dropping standards altogether. I simply have priorities that occasionally take precedence over personal grooming. Like eating. And brushing my teeth. And finding time to get to the toilet. After all, when you realise you've been busting to do a wee for the past six hours, you understand that taking two hours out to go to the hairdresser will be a long time away.

# I Knew My Standards Had Dropped When...

- ❤ I had worn the same outfit for three days in a row.
- ❤ I had worn the same socks for two days in a row.
- ❤ I had worn the same undies for two days in a row (but only because I slept in them and I hadn't showered yet).
- ❤ I dropped the kids at school in my pyjamas (which, given the tantalising risk that this would be the day the car would break down, was the most thrillingly dangerous moment of the week).
- ❤ I was still wearing maternity pants long after Toddler had her first birthday.
- ❤ My leg hair had grown long enough to plait.
- ❤ My last haircut was self-administered, in the bathroom, using a pair of nail scissors. As a result, my fringe was approximately five centimetres long, after the attempt to neaten and straighten got somewhat out of hand.
- ❤ I noticed a hair growing out of my face which had quite possibly been there for months.
- ❤ I used a home hair dye kit when my grey hairs began growing faster than I could pull them out. The kit did a wonderful job dyeing my hair. It also did a wonderful job dyeing my neck, my ears, my forehead, my bathroom, and an entire set of towels.
- ❤ I hadn't bothered with perfume for months, relying instead on that marvellously clean, refreshing 'baby wipes' scent.
- ❤ I decided that the smeared mascara left on my eyes from the previous day would work as a 'smoky eye' effect.
- ❤ My toenails and fingernails were nicely polished. However, as Toddler was the one administering the polish, so were my fingers and toes. In bright green. With sparkles.
- ❤ There was bolognaise sauce on my top. I hadn't served bolognaise in two days.
- ❤ There was pumpkin soup in my hair. I hadn't served pumpkin soup in a week.

# Caught with Your Standards Down

Not only is it highly likely that your standards will drop after you have kids, it is also exceedingly likely that you will be caught with your standards down by someone you want to impress.

Whether it's the girl from school who always made you feel inadequate, the ex-boyfriend who dumped you, the boy who never loved you (why, Josh Goldenbum? *Why?*), the friend who downgraded you, the teacher who gave you a hard time, the person who only saw you at your fattest/frumpiest/most immature . . . you are going to bump into them, and when you do, you are going to want to put your very best face forward. And inevitably, the exact opposite will happen.

I know. It's happened to me. I bumped into my old school teacher and was humiliated by my son who said, 'Whatever,' when told who she was. I bumped into a man I used to fancy with a crying Toddler in my arms and her dirty security blanket tying up my hair (in my defence, Toddler kept dropping it, and the day was very warm). And I bumped into an ex-boyfriend and felt I looked fantastic, until I glimpsed my reflection ten minutes later and found lettuce between my teeth.

| My Ideal Chance Meeting | My Real Chance Meeting |
|---|---|
| *I'm dressed casually but beautifully in some kind of impossibly hip outfit that I can't actually define because I can't actually imagine it.* | *I'm dressed in jeans, a shapeless T-shirt and thongs. Not the sexy kind of thong that you wear under your clothes. The tragic kind of thong that you wear on your feet.* |
| *My hair is perfectly styled, but 'messy' enough to show that it is effortless and always looks this way.* | *I have a ponytail in my hair (which hasn't been washed in over two weeks), kept in place with butterfly clips borrowed from Toddler.* |
| *My skin is flawless, line free, and glowing with good health and happiness.* | *My nose is shiny, there are bags under my eyes, and I have a pimple on a wrinkle.* |
| *I say 'hi' in an insouciant, sexy and confident voice.* | *I try to say 'hi' but am interrupted by Little Man yelling, 'Stop talking to that stupid man!' as Toddler shoves her fingers in my mouth.* |
| *My children are beautifully behaved.* | *My children are not beautifully behaved. See above.* |
| *I introduce my kids. They smile politely and give their names with ease.* | *I introduce my kids. When asked their names Pinkela answers, 'I don't know,' Little Man answers, 'SpongeBob Squarepants,' and Toddler answers, 'You're stoopid.'* |
| *I introduce The Architect. He shakes hands confidently and chats with wit and grace about his great love for me.* | *I introduce The Architect. He grunts and says he's going to go to the pastry shop.* |
| *We chat easily for several minutes, during which time it becomes clear that I am incredibly successful and happy.* | *We chat awkwardly for twenty seconds before I get hijacked by three marauding children and leave in shame.* |

# That Thing I (Don't) Do

*E*xercise is important. I know this. It makes you healthy. It keeps you fit. It gives you a boost of those happy hormones that you can otherwise only get from eating chocolate, and that you (used to) get from having sex. And it stops your thighs from doing that weird wobbly thing that they do. You know – like when your toddler comes up to you and places her hands on them and says, 'Look! Mummy all jiggly!'

Of course, these observations about exercise are purely theoretical. I wouldn't know for myself what exercise does because I can't actually remember. When you have young children, 'exercise' becomes something you do to the children to encourage them to sleep well at night; for example, making them run around the garden till they fall over. That kind of thing.

Now, health experts will tell you that exercise is vital, and that you just have to 'make time' for it. But how does one 'make time' exactly? You can't just 'make time' out of thin air. Only a certain number of hours in the day exist. And when you're up at the crack of dawn with little ones, busy all day with drop-offs and pick-ups and childcare and work and cooking and cleaning and running a household, and then up till late helping with homework and getting intractable kids off to sleep (my God, I'm exhausted just writing about it), well, that covers all available time.

There simply isn't any left.

Of course I could just take Toddler with me for power walks and the like. Sadly, however, she doesn't like sitting in her pram, and screams, 'Help! Help! Geddup!' until the other walkers become alarmed and look around for the authorities. And if I do allow her to get out of her pram, she runs very fast on her short little legs, which would be great, and I would run with her, were it not for the fact that she just runs in circles. Before falling down. Again and again.

To be honest, even if I did have a spare hour a day, I doubt I would spend it exercising. Exercise is simply not compatible with my lifestyle.

## Why Exercise Is Bad For Me

- ♀ *Exercise uses up time I could spend sleeping. At this point in my life, not even jiggly thighs can deter me from my primary goal, which is to spend as many precious moments unconscious as possible.*
- ♀ *Exercise only works in conjunction with sensible eating. Nutella, cappuccinos and leftover hot chips are hardly considered sensible.*
- ♀ *Managing to shower, dress myself, and dry my hair in the morning while wrangling Toddler and getting the big kids off to school is a mammoth achievement. To undo all that good work by getting hot and sweaty would just be silly.*
- ♀ *Gyms smell bad. I have to deal with enough bad smells at home. I don't need them when I'm out.*
- ♀ *The sight of very fit people makes me desperate to justify my wobbly tummy by explaining to all nearby that I've got three*

*children. This doesn't make them think that my stomach is less wobbly. It just makes them think that I am sad.*

♀ *I have sprained my neck just being in bed, and most days I trip over my own feet at least twice. The chances of getting through an exercise class or ball game unscathed are exceedingly slim.*

♀ *Exercising makes me hungry. I'm attempting to eat less food these days, not more.*

♀ *I'm outraged that pushing a pram and a trolley while wrangling a toddler and holding five shopping bags is not considered to be 'proper exercise'. I therefore refuse to do 'proper exercise' as a form of silent (if not especially powerful) protest.*

# Bag of Shame

*I* can't even remember what used to be in my handbag before I had kids. I'm fairly sure, however, that there weren't any baby wipes, I'm reasonably confident that there were no small toys, and I'm absolutely positive that there were no plastic-flavoured cheese sticks.

No doubt there was a fine assortment of goods, all designed to enhance the comfort of my own existence rather than stave off the mess created by others. I always did carry a lot of stuff. Still, before I had children, I used to clean my bag out regularly. It was satisfying to sort through all the junk accumulated over the past couple of weeks and start again with a fresh, neat handbag.

These days, I don't really clean out my bag. For one thing, I'm a busy working mother and I just don't have the time. For another thing, I have the tendency to use my handbag as an emergency waste receptacle, so I'm a little bit afraid of what I might discover.

## Reach Into My Bag and You'll Find

- My purse (empty).
- My keys.

❧ *An unwrapped tampon that has become all cute and fluffy.*

❧ *Several tampon wrappers.*

❧ *Used cotton buds.*

❧ *Clean toothpicks.*

❧ *Used toothpicks.*

❧ *Colourful swizzle sticks.*

❧ *Sachets of sweetener (stolen from various cafes).*

❧ *Sachets of salt (stolen from McDonald's).*

❧ *Chocolate mints (stolen from restaurants).*

❧ *Lollies (assorted, all of which have become unwrapped and fluffy from the open tampon).*

❧ *A very old cheese stick.*

❧ *A small bag of rice crackers, completely crushed.*

❧ *Several small toys.*

❧ *Several tiny pieces of small toys.*

❧ *A lipstick in its case.*

❧ *A lipstick without a case, also fluffy from the tampon.*

❧ *A ten-year-old pimple concealer stick (which never worked but provided comfort).*

❧ *Wrinkle cream (ditto).*

❧ *Various painkillers including those for headache, period pain, stomach-ache and backache.*

❧ *A Valium.*

❧ *Okay, two Valiums.*

❧ *Okay, two Valiums and a Xanax.*

❧ *Nailfiles.*

❧ *Bits of nail.*

❧ *Partially unwrapped plasters.*

❧ *Several shopping lists.*

❧ *Several discount vouchers, most long since expired.*

❧ *My mobile phone (which I can never find in the bag, but which doesn't matter as I never answer it, anyway).*

👙 Photos of my children (several years out of date).

👙 Used tissues.

👙 Baby wipes.

## Look Forever and You Still Won't Find

👠 A change of clothes for Toddler.

👠 A clean nappy.

👠 A wrapped tampon.

👠 Cash.

*Survival*

# Buy Me

*I* adore clothes shopping. It pleases me. Enormously. It soothes me when nothing else will. I may not be very good at shopping, I may end up returning (or hating) up to 50 per cent of my purchases (or more, after a particularly unsuccessful day of impulse buying), but I still love the act of shopping. With a passion.

Now, I know that not every woman loves shopping. I know that some women find clothes shopping to be rather burdensome. However, this, I believe, is due to a lack of funds, or lack of self-confidence, rather than an inherent flaw in the shopping paradigm. It is my deeply held belief that every woman – given enough money and a dress size they're happy with – has the potential to love shopping as passionately as I do. Clothes shopping, you see, is clearly the answer. And there doesn't even have to be a question.

As everybody knows, there are two types of shopping: the Needs-Driven Shop and the Impulse Buy.

The Needs-Driven Shop is a purposeful shop. I head to the shops when I have Nothing to Wear, whether to a cocktail party, a work function, the school speech night, or, if things are really dire, the supermarket.

There can be a certain agitation associated with the Needs-Driven Shop, given that time constraints are usually an issue. There is the constant temptation to buy the outfit that says 'Near Enough', rather than the one that screams 'You Complete Me!' Still, there is the satisfaction that comes from filling a gap, and the knowledge that although the sleeves are too short, the neckline too wide and the hemline a bit long, at least I won't be forced to wear that drop-waisted blue number I wore to my cousin's party three years ago.

The Impulse Buy is much more fun. I walk past a store and, despite having no pressing need for a sheer green kaftan studded with diamantés and purple beads, I buy it immediately because it is so unspeakably beautiful. (And no, I am not making that up. I actually do own a sheer green kaftan studded with diamantés and purple beads. And no, I do not know what I was thinking.) Of course, what I fail to appreciate is that the sheer green kaftan is unspeakably beautiful in the shop, on a hanger, among a bunch of other perfectly coordinated green and purple outfits. At home, on my actual body, standing in front of the mirror, it looks patently ridiculous.

The beauty of shopping is that the articles of clothing are, themselves, almost secondary to the pleasure of the act itself. Shopping stands alone as an intensely rewarding experience. So rewarding, in fact, that I find myself craving a purchase every few weeks (and more frequently in times of stress). Whether it's a jacket, frock, cardigan or cheap T-shirt, a new item in a bag serves to restore my equilibrium, at least until the next time I have Nothing to Wear.

## Why I Need to Shop

❧ Buying clothes for myself is one of the rare moments in my life when it is all about me. It's not about my kids. It's not about my work. It's not about The Architect. It's about me and what makes me happy. Oh, and what fits. Which can be an entirely different thing. But still...

❧ There's nothing better than seeing something before me, coveting it then transferring it to my possession. It is the most satisfying transaction possible. If gratification was always so easy, I wouldn't have had to pine in unrequited anguish for Josh Goldenbum all those years.

❧ Shopping gives me a rush of intense satisfaction that not only rivals an orgasm but – depending on the shop I am in and the limits of my budget – can be easier to achieve.

❧ Shopping can offer that thrill of illicit triumph. I hide my purchase in the car so that The Architect won't see it, smuggle it into the house when he's not at home, then wear it a week later and claim I bought it years ago, for only a third of the money that I actually spent. Ironically, The Architect is a bit of a spendthrift himself, and has no problem at all with me buying things; however, the need to play down my expenditure seems hardwired into me. I think it's genetic.

❧ Wearing my new outfit always brings me enormous pleasure. There is the intrinsic satisfaction of knowing I look good, but also all the compliments I receive from my friends and family. (And they do compliment me when they see me wearing something new, even if they don't particularly like it. That's just the polite thing to do.)

❧ If I decide later on I'm not happy with my purchase, I can return it for a refund or voucher. This is just like getting free money!

👠 *The mirrors in many clothes shops are incredibly flattering. I could live in some of those change rooms.*

👠 *The sales assistants in many clothes shops are incredibly flattering. Where else can I don a skin-tight fawn dress and be told that no one would ever know I've had three children?*

# Help Wanted

*E*veryone needs time-out from the kids once in a while. A month or two would be fabulous, but failing that, I'd settle for a few hours every second Saturday night. Time to catch up with friends, see a movie, go to a restaurant, maybe even have some alone time with The Architect (scary thought, I know). But to do any of that, I need a babysitter.

In an ideal world, my parents would babysit on a Saturday night. However, in my real world, my parents are, sadly, young, fit and popular, and have their own social arrangements on the weekend. So while they are delighted to spend time with their grandkids, it will never be on a Saturday evening when other opportunities may arise. Like the theatre. Or a party. Or attending a swingers' club. Who knows? I have absolutely no idea what they get up to in their spare time.

As a consequence, I must hire someone to look after my kids. And let me tell you, this is not easy. Of course, I could find *someone* to come and stay with my three children. It's just that finding a person who isn't scary, or twelve years old, or a religious fanatic, or likely to abscond in the middle of the night, is a somewhat harder task.

Finding a babysitter is the endless challenge of the parent of young kids; 'challenge' because they are hard to find, and 'endless' because even when you do find them they are likely to quit after a few months. Babysitters are a transient population, forever moving on to the first employer who offers a better salary and nicer kids. Which is why I never, ever share my babysitters with my friends. Because one minute I'm doing Karen a favour and letting her use my babysitter on a Sunday night, and the next thing you know, my babysitter is defecting to Karen's family, because Karen is willing to pay a pound an hour more, and Karen's kids don't stay up till ten p.m. demanding chocolate and bouncing on the beds. Like that's a big deal. I mean, *really*.

Still, my babysitters move on, just like everyone else's. So I have put together a job specification to make the recruitment process easier.

## Babysitter Needed

### Job description:

*To care for children in the absence of myself and The Architect (as we refuse to accept that our social lives are over just because we have children) or the grandparents (who have selfishly refused to give up their own social lives to babysit).*

### When:

*On Saturday nights. (Friday is for the family, and Sunday to Thursday are school nights. Besides, there is really good stuff on TV.)*

### Time:

*From seven till late (using 'late' in the sense of 'We're parents of young kids. By eight-thirty p.m. we're getting tired, by nine our eyes are becoming unfocused, by nine-thirty we're congratulating each other on how late we've stayed out, and by ten we're heading home).*

## Duties:

**7.00:** *Greet children with enthusiasm. Reassure them that they can finish watching their DVD.*

**7.05:** *Greet me with enthusiasm. Reassure me that I look nice, and that the spaghetti splotch on my sleeve is hardly noticeable.*

**7.10:** *Greet The Architect, with or without enthusiasm. (In fact, if you are extremely attractive, enthusiasm is discouraged. We wouldn't want to raise the poor guy's hopes.)*

**7.20:** *Reassure me of your knowledge of emergency numbers and procedures.*

**7.25:** *Reassure me that the watermelon stain on my top is hardly noticeable, either.*

**7.30:** *Prise the kids off me and The Architect and stand with them at the front door cheerily waving goodbye.*

**7.35–10.30:** *Start by playing a game of Monopoly. Move on to a round of Twister. Read Toddler a book while Little Man and Pinkela play Wii. Pour all three kids glasses of milk and offer them last-minute snacks. Take Toddler to the toilet and ensure that all three kids have brushed their teeth. Tuck the kids into... Oh, who am I kidding? To be honest, I don't care if the four of you stand on the balcony and howl at the moon for the next three hours, so long as the house is tidy and the kids are asleep when we get home.*

## Essential Criteria:

- *Love of children, particularly those who eat with their fingers, rub food into each other's hair, make bottom jokes, and bounce on the couch till ten p.m.*

- *Sense of humour (to laugh again and again at those wonderful bottom jokes).*

*Kerri Sackville*

- Excellent conflict resolution skills (to settle conflicts arising between Little Man and Pinkela, between you and the children, or between The Architect and me as we're heading out the door).
- Excellent crisis management skills (to deal with tantrums, minor accidents, and those times when conflict resolution doesn't work).
- Ability to get kids to do what you want (also known as 'bribery').
- Competence in teeth brushing (the children's teeth, not your own, but personal dental hygiene is, of course, highly regarded).
- Selective deafness (believe me, you'll need it when those bottom jokes kick in).
- Selective blindness (so I don't feel the need to clean up before you arrive).
- Selective muteness (so you don't tell everyone about my messy home and naughty kids).
- Punctuality. (After all, when those precious minutes of freedom are ticking away I can get a little cranky.)
- Reliability. (Oh, please don't cancel. Pleeease! I want to have fun!)

**Desirable criteria:**

- Good looks (my kids love pretty girls) but not excessively good looks (The Architect loves pretty girls, too).
- No friends. (We wouldn't want you being tempted by invitations to go out partying on a Saturday night.)
- Extensive general knowledge (so that I can refer all those pesky little questions like, 'Mummy, where does gravity come from?' straight to you).
- Your own car (so that we don't have to argue over whose responsibility it is to take you home – or, if you are excessively good-looking, whose right it is to take you home).

*If you meet these criteria and wish to apply for the position, please give me a call.*

*And if you don't meet these criteria and wish to apply for the position, please give me a call anyway. We're desperate to go out and, quite frankly, we'll take anyone.*

# Adults' Night Out

*I* get terribly excited when I'm going out with my friends. This is partly because I really, really love my friends, and partly because I spend most of my time either with three children under the age of twelve, or alone at a computer, and any company that is not a child or electronic is a great treat for me.

Now, obviously before any night out I have to do a bit of preparation. I merrily note the date on my calendar (among notes like 'Year Three parent–teacher meeting', 'Car tax expires' and 'Mika's 2nd B-day party'), book a babysitter, and immediately begin planning my outfit. Oh, don't get me wrong – it's not that I have so many clothes to choose from – it's just that I don't dress up to hang out with kids and sit alone at the computer, so wearing a proper outfit is rather a big deal.

Now, sometimes I just pick out the outfit, make sure it's clean, and hang it up, ready for the big night. Sometimes I actually try it on, accessorise, and do a strut in front of the mirror. Always, by the time I am finished, I know that I have chosen well and that I will look great on the night.

And then the night arrives. And, somehow, everything is different.

I don my carefully chosen outfit, confidently, and with anticipation. And, to my horror and despair, it is wrong. All wrong. Though just weeks, if not days, ago it made me look svelte and effortlessly stylish, today it makes me look short, dumpy and hideously old.

What has happened in the intervening time? How did something so right go so horribly wrong? Did I change? Did my mirrors change? Did the outfit undergo some subtle transformation, a minute reconfiguration of details that turned the sublime into the ridiculous?

Now, I know that I could just leave the outfit on and concentrate on having a good time, but as any woman knows, I just can't *have* a good time if I know I look like crap. So it's time for Option Two.

We've all experienced Option Two.

Option Two involves running around agitatedly for several minutes, rummaging through the contents of my wardrobe, running my fingers through my hair, and glancing anxiously at the clock as I desperately try to find a replacement outfit.

Option Two involves The Architect walking into the room, telling me edgily that I look 'fine' in whichever of the outfits I happen to be wearing at that exact moment, and reminding me firmly that we're already fifteen minutes late and that it's time to get moving.

Option Two involves me accepting that if there's any chance of us actually making it to our function, I'm going to have to give up my search for the Perfect Outfit and just go with the Next Best Thing. So I look into the mirror at my Whichever Outfit and These-Will-Have-to-Do Shoes, sigh deeply, and duck into the bathroom to apply my make-up, where I stuff up my mascara and get lipstick on my teeth in my hurry to get out the door, and have no time to do my hair as The Architect hauls me out to the car.

Then we go and meet my friends, none of whom even

notice my outfit, as most are still recovering from their own adventures in Getting Ready, and are all a bit drunk anyway. So I relax, put a glass in my hand, and have a great time.

Until I get home and notice my frizzy hair, my smudged mascara, and the fact that my brown shoes look completely ridiculous with my black dress, and I feel like a right fool.

## Leaving the House: A Timeline

**6.00:** We have a dinner reservation with friends for eight p.m. at a restaurant approximately fifteen minutes away. There is tons of time to get ready. I feel relaxed and am looking forward to a fun night out.

**6.10:** I make the kids frankfurters and noodles for dinner.

**6.20:** The kids announce that they don't like frankfurters and noodles, despite having requested them for dinner every single night for the past five years.

**6.25:** I tell the kids it's either frankfurters and noodles for dinner, or nothing. They choose nothing.

**6.30:** The babysitter arrives.

**6.31:** Toddler runs wailing down the corridor and clings pathetically to my legs shouting, 'Go way, Kath! No Kath! Kath is stoopid!'

**6.32:** The older kids greet the babysitter cheerily and announce that they are starving, because, 'Mum didn't let us have any dinner!' The babysitter looks concerned, although I am not sure whether this is due to the crying Toddler or the fact that I have deprived my children of food.

**6.40:** I give in to the babysitter's unspoken words of judgement, make Little Man a Vegemite sandwich and give Pinkela a can of tuna, and tell the babysitter to help herself to the frankfurters.

**6.50:** *Toddler is still clinging to my leg. I search for The Architect only to find him in the bedroom, reclining peacefully on the bed. I deposit Toddler firmly on his lap.*

**7.00:** *I step into the shower.*

**7.01:** *Toddler barges into the shower pleading for a bottle. I call to The Architect to get the bottle. There is no answer. My husband is clearly far too busy reclining on the bed to respond.*

**7.02:** *I get out of the shower, having barely moistened myself, let alone managed to use soap or shampoo. I wrap myself in a towel, and fetch Toddler her bottle.*

**7.07:** *I plonk Toddler rather firmly on The Architect's lap again.*

**7.09:** *I put on the outfit I had planned to wear. It looks hideous. I can't believe I even considered wearing such a ridiculous and unflattering combination of clothes.*

**7.10:** *I remove the outfit and look in my wardrobe for a nice alternative.*

**7.15:** *I realise with mounting panic that I have Nothing to Wear. I run around agitatedly, throwing items of clothing on the bed, until I have a pile the size of a small tree, and still no idea what to wear.*

**7.25:** *With shame and regret, I settle for the same top and trousers I have worn the last three times I have been out to dinner with these particular friends.*

**7.30:** *I look in the mirror and realise there is a smudge of something Toddler-like on the front of my top. I try to wipe it off with my bath towel.*

**7.35:** *I realise with horror that my efforts have simply spread the smudge, quite significantly really. I give up and hope that the lighting in the restaurant is very dim.*

**7.37:** *I realise we need to be at the restaurant in twenty-three minutes. I ask The Architect to get dressed. He mutters something about 'in a sec'.*

**7.38:** *I lift Toddler off The Architect, take her to her room, and attempt to put her to bed.*

**7.40:** *Toddler cries loudly. I pat her for ten minutes, before firmly closing the door to the mournful sounds of, 'Mama! Mama!' coming from the bedroom.*

**7.50:** *I ask The Architect to get dressed. He mutters something about 'Stop nagging me'.*

**7.52:** *I check on the children who are playing happily with the babysitter. There is mess all over the kitchen. I decide to leave it.*

**7.55:** *I put on my make-up. Unfortunately I close my eyes just a little too early and end up with a mascara trail down my face.*

**8.00:** *I scrub off my eye make-up and begin to reapply it. Looking up, I notice the time, think better of it, and give up. I guess I'll just have to make do with lip gloss and a smile.*

**8.05:** *I ask The Architect to get dressed. He sighs heavily and mutters something about how demanding I am. My smile disappears. I guess I'll just have to make do with lip gloss.*

**8.07:** *I say goodbye to the children. Suddenly they are desperate not to see me leave. 'Please, Mum, don't go,' Little Man begs. 'Don't leave us!' cries Pinkela. I prise them off my legs and head to the door.*

**8.10:** *I am still waiting at the door. The Architect strolls nonchalantly down. 'Ready?' he asks. I scowl.*

**8.11:** *In the car, two streets away, I realise I have forgotten my mobile phone. I briefly consider remaining out of contact for the evening, but visions of fire and ambulances pop into my head. I reluctantly instruct The Architect to turn back.*

**8.12:** *As I enter the house, my kids see me and cheer. 'Mummy's home!' shouts Pinkela. 'Hooray!' shouts Little Man. 'Mama?' calls Toddler from her room. I rush upstairs, grab my phone and run outside again.*

**8.15:** *We are finally on our way. I sit, agitated, mobile phone in hand, knowing we are going to be at least half an hour late.*

**8.17:** *The phone rings. It is Pinkela, asking if she can have chocolate milk. I say yes.*

**8.19:** *The phone rings. It is Little Man, asking if he can play more Game Boy. I say no.*

**8.31:** *We arrive at the restaurant, panting and frazzled. We look around for our friends. They are not here.*

**8.35:** *Our friends call. 'Sorry, we're running a bit late,' they say. 'Trouble with the kids...'*

# Mums Go Off

Sometimes it's not enough just to get away from your children. Sometimes, you also need to get away from your partner. And for this reason, the girls' night out is of critical importance.

Now, there are many things I have learned since becoming a mother. Probably not as many as I *should* have learned (I do spend a little too much time playing with Twitter and watching shows starring Simon Baker), but still, there are a few. I have learned that mince is the world's most versatile meat. I have learned that baby powder removes oil stains from clothing. I have learned that you can love a child passionately and still long for time away from them.

And I have learned that no one parties as hard, no one laughs as loudly, no one flirts with the twenty-year-old waiters quite as outrageously, as a group of middle-aged mothers on evening leave from home.

Every few months, I go to dinner with five of my girlfriends, the women from my original mothers' group. We have been together as a group since our first babies were born, and don't manage to all meet up nearly as often as we'd like, so our girls' nights out are very special. And they all follow a predictable pattern.

We arrive at the restaurant. One of us will arrive as planned at seven-thirty – either because her kids have been exceptionally well behaved (so that she can escape early), or because her kids have been exceptionally badly behaved (so that she absconds as soon as her husband walks in the door). The rest of us will trickle in over the next hour, according to what time our husbands get home, how quickly we can peel our kids off our legs, and whether or not we can find anything to wear.

The evening starts with hugs and kisses all round, followed by comments on how we are all looking. Most comments are complimentary ('Love the top!', 'Ooh, great shoes, honey!' or 'Oh, I adore that colour on you!'), and thus must be instantly rebutted ('Oh, this old thing? I've had it for ages' or 'Really? I'm not so sure I like it'), because God forbid we should take a compliment graciously.

Occasionally the comments are less than flattering, but this is always out of concern. 'Are you okay? You look tired' is, of course, code for 'You're really not looking so hot tonight', but it paves the way for conversation about how crap things are, so it serves a useful function.

Once conversation is flowing it is time for drinks. We start with a round of cocktails, which gets us nicely in the mood to party, as we are all tragic lushes who get sloshed at the sight of a triangular glass on a stem.

It's then that the fun really begins. We laugh, a lot. We talk loudly, about everyone we know (using 'everyone we know' in the sense of 'our husbands'). We discuss our kids, our breasts, our parents, our jobs, our grievances, and our various health ailments. We converse about politics, literature, climate change, and the arts. (Nah, not really. I just put that in to see if you were paying attention.) We eat – a great deal, in fact – from our own and each other's plates. We flirt wildly with the waiters (which is, admittedly, a bit sad, but they're paid to put up with it and they generally keep a brave face).

As the night continues, we get happier and happier – a combination of being child-free, husband-free, responsibility-free and, you know, *drunk* – and things get even more exciting. We start telling each other how much we love each other. We make speeches about our friendships. We try to flirt with the men at adjoining tables (which is more than a little bit sad, and makes them look kind of terrified).

Then we start talking about our sex lives (or lack thereof), and one of us nearly falls off her chair, and another one laughs so hard her cocktail comes out of her nose, and things really start to kick off.

And then suddenly, someone exclaims, 'Oh my God, look how late it is! I have to get home to bed!'

We all look at our watches. It is ten-thirty. My God! We can't believe we've stayed up this late. We are exhausted! We pay the bill, say our goodbyes, wave cheekily to the waiters, nod sheepishly to the men at the next tables, and leave, vowing to do it all again very soon.

We mothers party very hard. We mothers party very loudly.

But we mothers party very, very fast.

# Up, Up and Away!

*O*f course, getting away from the kids for a few hours of an evening is lovely. However, the ultimate escape is to get away from the kids for an entire weekend, or – how I sigh just thinking of it – a week or two.

Now, getting rid of all three of my kids at once (I mean, er, securing *alternative care* for all three of my kids at once) is fairly challenging. It's not like I can just fill up the fridge, leave a few pounds on the kitchen bench, kiss them goodbye, and take off on a holiday. There are arrangements to be made, carers to be found, helpers to assist the carers, schedules and plans and lists to be drawn up to enable the helpers to assist the carers... Honestly, it's exhausting. If I didn't really need a holiday before I started planning one, I certainly will by the time we head to the airport.

Now, happily for me, my parents have agreed to take my children on several occasions so that The Architect and I can get away for a break. This is partly because they adore my kids and want to spend time with them, and partly because they love me and want to help me out. Mostly, however, it is because they feel guilty about never babysitting on a Saturday night. As indeed they should.

Once you've been a parent for a year or two, travelling

without your kids becomes a rare and precious experience. Of course, travelling *with* your kids is awesome too (using 'awesome' in the sense of 'breathtaking to watch the flight attendant remove an entire aeroplane seat after your son throws up all over it'). However, as we know, it isn't what one would refer to as 'relaxing'.

Travelling without kids gives you the chance to actually stop being a parent for a period of time (provided you turn your mobile phone off for twenty-three hours of the day). And it allows you to do all those things you can't do when you're a busy mother, such as sleeping, going to the toilet alone, and ... that's pretty much it.

And that's exactly what I want to do every time I go away without the kids. *Nothing.* Unfortunately, The Architect doesn't agree. He thinks that travel is for 'travelling', an activity which clearly requires exertion and energy – quite the opposite of what I plan to have. So while he gets fired up, planning sightseeing expeditions, day tours, canoeing, diving, trips to remote beaches and kava drinking ceremonies, I start fantasising about being prone on a bed. I work hard all year looking after the kids and the house and the man – not to mention fitting in work every spare second – and in my time off I want to relax and do absolutely nothing. Zero. Nil. Zilch. Nada.

Oh, okay. I'm exaggerating. I don't really want to do nothing. I want to eat, of course. I want to read. I want to watch TV. I want to have long baths and flick through fashion magazines. I want to have a massage and lie in the sun. And I want to ... no, nothing else really, unless sleeping counts as something?

Of course, one may ask why I need to get on a plane and fly to a holiday location when I could have a bath and lie on a bed reading magazines just as easily here at home.

Well, it's just not the same thing.

You see, I love travelling to new cities and faraway coun-tries. I love experiencing different places, cultures and people. I just find that the best way to experience them is through the medium of food, room service and television.

What's more, I can be *found* in this country, recalled home in a few hours in the case of an unexpected crisis – which, given that I have three kids, is reasonably likely. It's much harder to bring me back from a place accessible only by boat, bus and a long-distance flight. My parents and the kids will just have to cope without me.

Sadly, though, my husband refuses to do absolutely noth-ing for the whole five days. He likes to do really annoying things, like go for walks, swim in the pool, and leave our hotel to look at the local sights. Apparently it is important to actu-ally 'see' the place you are visiting. Ridiculous.

Still, even he can't rouse me during the long-distance flight. It may be cramped, the food may be crappy, and I may be uncomfortable, but at least I'll have nothing to do but sleep.

# Guilt Trip

*U*nfortunately, travelling without kids comes with a price, and I'm not just talking about the cost of the airline tickets and the hotel.

The price is guilt.

Once the tickets are booked, the arrangements have been made, and the suitcases are packed, I generally feel overwhelmed with anticipation, using 'anticipation' in its common maternal sense of 'guilt and anxiety'.

Not that anything will go wrong, but what if something goes wrong? For a start, the kids obviously pine for us terribly every time we go away. The last time I broke the news to them that they were going to Nana and Papa's so that we could go on holidays, they seemed deeply traumatised. Okay, so Toddler seemed to take it well (actually, she started singing 'Happy Birthday to Nana', which I assumed was a good sign), but Little Man was clearly distressed. 'How will I play Game Boy?' he asked me fretfully.

'You can take Game Boy with you,' I told him. 'And you can even play an extra ten minutes per day.'

'Yippee!' he shouted, punching the air. 'Extra Game Boy! When are you leaving?'

Still, Pinkela was genuinely heartbroken. 'Where are you going?' she asked, looking soulfully at me with her big eyes. 'How long will you be away? Who will look after me? Will you bring me a present?'

'On holidays, for a week, Nana and Papa, and of course I'll bring you a present,' I told her. 'A big one.'

'Yippee!' she shouted, punching the air. 'Presents! When are you leaving?'

Even if the kids don't pine as much as ... er ... expected (and really, I'm sure they were just trying to spare my feelings), there are still all sorts of things to worry about. Every aspect of my children's daily lives involves careful planning and preparation and timing, and if Nana gets any of it wrong, their whole routine could descend into chaos.

There is school to be driven to on time, with lunches, homework books and sports clothes packed in bags. Homework to be completed and handed in the next day. Instruments to be practised for ten minutes each afternoon. Swimming, karate, and dance lessons to attend, with towels/karate outfit/dance shoes in tow.

And then there is the food. Oh my God, how I lose sleep about food. What if my kids don't eat healthily while I'm away? Or worse, what if they don't eat at all? True, in Pinkela's case this is highly unlikely, but Little Man and Toddler could quite happily exist on cheese and chocolate for a week at a time. And believe me, there'll be chocolate. My parents believe that when the grandchildren are in their care, they can feed them whatever they want (or, in other words, buy their everlasting love with treats). Well, this is very nice, and I'm in favour of family ties, and there's nothing at all wrong with ice-cream every night for a week. But then I come home, and not only do the kids resent me for going away, I also look like the bad guy for refusing to offer dessert after every meal!

No, it's all way too difficult, I realise. I can't possibly leave my children. I'm a parent, I have responsibilities, I can't go gallivanting around the world. So I make a decision. We'll just have to take the kids with us.

And then I think about how exhausted I feel, and a vision of white hotel sheets floats serenely before my eyes. Yes, we'll take the kids with us on holidays. Using 'kids' in the sense of 'guilt and anxiety'.

Children, we'll see you in a week. Dad and I are on our way!

# Lost in Fantasy

Motherhood can be fairly mundane. (Oh, who am I kidding? Motherhood can be *totally* mundane.) And – although I adore my kids and wouldn't give them up for the world (except perhaps from six o'clock every Saturday night until ten o'clock Sunday morning) – I fantasise regularly about a life less mundane, where fantastical things happen, and all ordinariness is swept away.

The thing is, mothers fantasise. Hell, *women* fantasise. But I think that the more restrictions we experience in our real lives, the more likely we are to fantasise about breaking free from those restrictions and living the life – or part of the life – we are unable to live. It's like craving chocolate when you're on a diet. You might normally be able to take or leave a block of Cadbury's, but when you know it's off limits it's enticing beyond belief.

So what are my fantasies? What are the imaginary scenarios that drive me wild with their promises of delight, that envelop me in the supermarket as I place washing powder in my trolley, that transport me far away as I wipe bottoms and make school lunches, and that elevate me to (even) greater heights as I have sex with my husband?

## *My Top Ten Daydreams*

1. *I have some quality Alone Time. Now, when I say Alone Time I mean proper Alone Time – not just an hour, or an afternoon, or even a full day, but a week, or a month, or even two. Quality Alone Time, with no work, no kids, no housework and no responsibilities. Time to pursue nothing but the fulfilment of my own desires. Time to read. Have massages. Go for walks. Drink cocktails. Watch endless re-runs of The Mentalist. Take long bubble baths while drinking champagne. Eat cheeseburgers and hot chips in bed. And sleep. For twelve hours. Or a whole day. Or even two.*

2. *I have a brilliantly successful boob job, without any of the costs involved, the risks of surgery, or the side effects (except for the part where I end up with nice, perky breasts). Ditto liposuction, full face lift, and any other anti-ageing procedures on offer.*

3. *My metabolism changes dramatically, so that I become one of those naturally skinny people who struggles to gain weight. Desperately, I eat pancakes for breakfast, hot chips between meals, jars of Nutella as snacks, and creamy pastas every evening. And I only manage to stay a size six.*

4. *I win the lottery. Not just a little bit of money. Masses. Like, millions and millions of pounds. Enough to pay off our house, get fabulous new cars, go on a luxury holiday, buy wardrobes full of designer clothes, give lots and lots to every possible worthy charity ... and then here my brain sort of stops because I have no idea what I would do with the rest of it. Still, I'm sure I would work it out. Quite sure. Truly. Bring it on.*

5. *I get home-cooked dinners delivered to my door every night. Actually, make that home-cooked breakfasts, lunches and dinners delivered to my door every day and night. In fact, why not just have a full-time chef living discreetly in our kitchen*

*(which is large, of course, after being redone following our lottery win). He can be kept company by our...*

6. Full-time housekeeper, who arrives first thing in the morning and leaves last thing at night when every dish has been put away, the clothes have been washed, ironed and returned to their rightful wardrobes, the beds have been made, and the house is sparkling clean.

7. My children go on a month-long camp (using 'month' in the sense of 'six or seven weeks') from which they return happy, stimulated, well educated, fit, polite, respectful, and clamouring to go back.

8. I write a bestselling book. A massive bestseller. Harry Potterish. I get worldwide fame and acclaim, and make lots and lots of money (possibly negating the need for the lottery win, but I can always give more to charity). I appear on all the talk shows, and I get to sign lots and lots of books. I'm not sure why I want to sign books, but that's just always sounded fun.

9. I win an Academy Award for Best Screenplay. Now, I haven't actually written a screenplay, and I have no interest in writing one. However, I want to win an Academy Award, and as I am unlikely to win an Oscar for Best Actress (if you had seen the miniseries I starred in, you would know why), this seems the most likely way to get one. I wear a stunning dress (probably something silvery and mesh, but that changes from week to week), receive an incredible goodie bag containing jewels and watches and – I have no idea, what do those goodie bags contain? – and make a witty, emotive and yet succinct speech, all without being ushered off the stage by the orchestra. Oh, and Simon Baker presents the award. Of course. Which is how...

10. I have sex with Simon Baker. When he meets me at the Academy Awards, the chemistry is instant, and overwhelming. He takes me back to his hotel room. We make passionate love. Simon

*rings his wife and informs her that he is leaving her. I ring my husband and say the same. My husband fully understands, says he wants to remain best friends, and that he will care for the children and be there for me anytime I wish to return. 'Stay a week, a month, even a year,' he says. 'It's Simon Baker! My God, who can blame you?' So I do.*

## *Epilogue*

# *So Is It All Worth It?*

$S$o here's the thing. If I was writing The Architect's and my love story, it would be deeply romantic. It would begin with our meeting at university, move through our intense teenage relationship, progress to the complication of our break-up, peak with our passionate reunion, and conclude with our beautiful wedding.

But this book isn't The Architect's and my love story. It's about what comes after the love story. And what comes after the love story isn't always romantic. It's often tedious and mundane. It's washing dishes and going to weekend sports and making school lunches and paying bills. It's buying toilet paper and brushing teeth and cleaning the fridge and going to the doctor. It's being selfless. It's putting other people's needs before my own. And it's doing a whole lot of things I don't really want to do.

So what's keeping me here? Is it all worth it?

Well, yes, of course it is. For one thing, I love my husband. He can make me crazy, and often does. He can make me furious, and we argue a lot. But at the end of the day, I love him. I miss him when he's away. I like it when he comes home. I like chatting to him, watching TV with him, laughing with him, exchanging banter. I like getting into our bed when he's already in it. I don't want to be without him.

And I love our kids. Achingly. When Toddler runs up to me and holds my face in her two hands and gives me a huge wet kiss and cries, 'I love you too, Mummy!', I could explode with joy. The child is bliss, pure bliss. Every time I pick her up from crèche, every time I lift her out of her cot, every time I fetch her from her Nana's house, it is like seeing her for the first time.

And Pinkela makes my heart sing with pride. She is a truly beautiful person, both inside and out. With all her dreaminess, with all her forgetfulness, she is the closest thing to perfection I have known. I cannot believe I created her.

As for my Little Man, well, he owns me. He is my firstborn, and my only son. He is special, in so many ways, and his insights, his intelligence, and his sensitivity tear at my soul. When he is happy, all is right in my world.

My husband and children are the cornerstones of my universe, and I still cannot believe how blessed I have been. And yet these feelings coexist nicely with the frequent urge to run screaming from the house, throw up my hands, and be alone for a week or ten.

My family delight, frustrate, enrich and exhaust me.

And I look forward to them doing so for the rest of my life.

*Bibliography*

# Books We Wish Were on the Shelf

➘ *Yes, Dear!: Creating Positive Husbands*

➘ *Yes, Mum!: Creating Obedient Children*

➘ *Speed Sleeping: How to Fully Rejuvenate in Three Minutes*

➘ *Telepathic Cleaning: Make That Mess Disappear Using Only the Power of Your Mind*

➘ *Body after Baby: How to Lose Weight Without Diet, Exercise, or in Fact Making Any Lifestyle Changes Whatsoever*

➘ *Mother's Little Helper: 50 Legal Herbs to Help You Get Through the Day*

➘ *Do-It-Yourself Face Lift: Plastic Surgery at Home!*

➘ *100 Ways with Frankfurters*

➘ *100 Ways with Maternity Jeans*

➘ *100 Ways with Headless Barbies*

➘ *100 Ways with Baby Wipes*

➘ *100 Ways with Single Socks*

➘ *100 Meals That Won't Stain, Smear or Crumble*

➘ *100 Highly Effective Fantasies for Use During Marital Sex*

➘ *100 Places Where Your Missing Keys Will Be*

➘ *How to Subtly Ditch Friends Without Alienating People*

*Even More About Me*

## Life and Other Crises

*F*or more about Him, Them and Me, check out three of my most popular blog posts at www.lifeandothercrises.blogspot.com:

Simon Says Sex

Three Girls Make Contact with a Man with Magic Hands

Tomorrow I Am Taking a Lover

*The Meatball Song*

Ke$ha's 'Tik Tok' was playing on the radio and it profoundly irritated me. Who on earth wakes up 'feeling like P. Diddy'? Most of the time I wake up with Toddler tugging my arm and demanding her chocky milk. And I certainly wouldn't be 'hitting this city' any time soon, either. Not with three kids in tow.

'Wake up in the morning feeling like Mummy,' I muttered to myself. I heard my children in the playroom blasting the TV.

Hey, that rhymed! Hmm ... I had an idea.

I ran to the computer. Of course, it was five-thirty and I should have been cooking dinner, but this was far more fun. The kids joined me and contributed as I started to type, furiously, new lyrics to the 'Tik Tok' song. Lyrics that I could relate to. Lyrics that mothers everywhere could relate to.

I posted the lyrics on my blog, and was inundated with 6,000 (okay, six) requests for me to make a film clip. So with the help of my Twitter friend Adam, my kids, the most advanced Auto Tune technology available, and some felafel posing as meatballs, I did.

And 'The Meatball Song' was born. Enjoy.

# Thank You

To my Twitter buddies. This book would not have existed without you.

To Lana Hirschowitz, for everything you have contributed to this book, and to my life.

To Mia Freedman, an inspiration in harem jeans, for all your help along the way.

To Pippa Masson, my gorgeous agent, for taking such great care of me.

To the Robson Press team, especially Iain Dale, for his overwhelming enthusiasm, and for making this book the best it could be.

To Mandy, Lisa, Carol, Ingrid, Janine and Adam, Karen and Greg, and Jodie and John, for the love, the laughter, and the endless material.

To my parents, for your unwavering support, and for your amazing strength in recent years.

To my kids, for giving me a life worth writing about.

And to Tony, for encouraging me to do it.

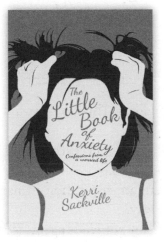